PETER LEONE'S
Show Jumping
Clinic

Storey Publishing

Peter Leone's Show Jumping Clinic

SUCCESS STRATEGIES FOR EQUESTRIAN ATHLETES

Peter Leone and Kimberly S. Jaussi, PhD

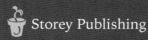 Storey Publishing

*The mission of Storey Publishing is to serve our customers by
publishing practical information that encourages
personal independence in harmony with the environment.*

Edited by Lisa H. Hiley and Deborah Burns
Art direction and book design by Carolyn Eckert
Text production by Theresa E. Wiscovitch

Cover photography by © Arnd Bronkhorst/www.arnd.nl (front) and © Mark Morris (back)
Interior photography credits appear on page 206
Illustrations by Jean Abernethy, except for © Janet Crawford: 64, and Joanna Rissanen:
    36 (right) and 70. Original sketch for 36 (left) by Steve Milne.
Arena diagrams and other graphics by Ilona Sherratt

Indexed by Susan Olason

Storey Publishing
210 MASS MoCA Way
North Adams, MA 01247
www.storey.com

Printed in China by Toppan Leefung Printing Ltd.
10 9 8 7 6 5 4 3 2 1

Library of Congress Cataloging-in-Publication Data

Leone, Peter, 1960–
 Peter Leone's show jumping clinic / by Peter Leone and Kimberly S. Jaussi.
    p. cm.
 Includes index.
 ISBN 978-1-60342-717-3 (hardcover w/ jacket : alk. paper)
 1. Show jumping. 2. Show jumping—Technique. 3. Show horses—Training.
 I. Jaussi, Kimberly S., 1966– II. Title.
 SF295.5.L46 2012
 798.2'5079—dc23
                     2011051311

Dr. and Mrs. Leone at CSIO Lucerne, Switzerland, 1982

To my family, who inspired my love of sport, competition, and horses:

My wife, Marcella, and children, Christina and Peter, Jr., who understand and support all the time and dedication I give to my profession;

My brothers, who spent countless hours with me after school and in the summers, riding, playing, and trying to beat each other;

My mother, medical professor and horsewoman, whose love and guidance made me the rider and teacher I am today;

And my father, who gave me the deep rooted belief that I could achieve anything I set my mind to. — P L

To my family, friends, teachers, and coaches, who have supported and encouraged me throughout the years to reach for my dreams, never give up, follow my heart, help others learn and develop, and strive to make an impact. You know who you are. I love you. And to my children, Maia and Peter, who together keep my well of inspiration overflowing. — K J

Peter Leone on
Select winning
the 2010 Devon
Grand Prix

Foreword

GEORGE MORRIS

SHORTLY AFTER I MOVED my training operation to New Jersey in 1971, I started noticing three energetic boys riding their ponies on the local horseshow circuit. They were students of Sullivan Davis, a great horseman who taught them the fundamentals. A few years later, Dr. Armand Leone, the boys' father, asked if I would take them on as they moved up the ranks. I was delighted to welcome these athletic, hard-working young men to my program. They were full of talent and the whole family was deeply dedicated to the sport. They were competitive too: If one boy had to have a hunter, the other two did as well. If one had to have an equitation horse, so did the others!

I enjoyed watching and nurturing their different styles: Armand was an intellectual, aggressive rider; Peter was the emotional and sensitive one, with a real feeling for his horses; and Mark was more laid back and intuitive in his approach. They all developed into outstanding riders and I was very proud of all of them, but it has been particularly gratifying to see Peter become a teacher and trainer. My job is primarily that of teacher and I'm always pleased when my students take what they've learned from me and from other trainers and pass it along to another generation.

In life, as well as in show jumping and other careers, you need three essential teachers. The first teaches you the basics (in Peter's case, this was Sullivan Davis) and the second provides the technical training to hone your skills. I was honored to play that role for Peter before sending him along to the third level, where coaches like Bert DeNemethy, Frank Chapot, and Michael Matz shared their world-class experience and helped Peter reach the top of his profession.

Jumping is not just a physical sport — it is also mental, emotional, and spiritual. Peter understands this well and his teaching is enriched by his emotional connection to his horses, his concern for their wellbeing, and his commitment to the principles of classical riding. In this book, he and coauthor Kim Jaussi distill Peter's decades of experience — both in the saddle and learning from the best — and present his own interpretation of time-honored techniques and concepts. They have filtered and condensed that experience in a lively and compelling way so that readers can feel that they've taken a clinic from one of the top riders, coaches, and trainers in the sport. I think any rider will benefit from the knowledge, experience, and insight contained here.

Peter Leone
on Select,
Winter
Equestrian
Festival,
Wellington,
Florida, 2010

Introduction

WELCOME TO AN INSIDE LOOK at riding, training, and showing in the world of competitive jumping. While the basic principles of correctly riding and training horses have not altered over the past century, the questions and challenges of our sport have changed dramatically.

Mastering the fundamental principles, established over the centuries, remains critical to our ability to ride, train, manage, and set goals successfully in today's sport. We wrote this book to familiarize you with the absolute and time-tested truths and principles of riding and jumping, and to guide you in using them to succeed today and as our sport moves into the future. Our philosophy is based on using the tried-and-true basics of communicating with a horse — the fundamental principles of classical riding and horsemanship — to answer the questions in horse sports and equally important, the new questions of tomorrow.

The essential keys to riding a horse never change, only the questions we have to answer. The more skilled we are in historically correct and classical riding, and the better we are at understanding the questions today's sport poses, the better we can answer them successfully and consistently — in other words, win!

We recommend reading from beginning to end, as each chapter builds on the material presented in the previous ones. Once read, you can refer to any part of the book for specific principles, tips, and exercises. While acknowledging that there is not "one right way" to train a horse and rider, we do feel that there are a number of universal principles that hold true across different riding and training systems. In addition to sharing these principles, we discuss the training and riding systems that we have learned from masters of the sport and that have helped us throughout our careers in riding. In Peter's case, that includes succeeding at the highest levels, up to an Olympic medal in show jumping and a distinguished international career in riding, training, and coaching.

Take your time to read the book, internalize the information, and then personalize it to work for you. Riding and training horses is a lifelong process — it's up to you to keep the process moving forward. Build on what you learn, always keep learning, and use your knowledge to take you to an even better place. The principles and knowledge garnered over the years will provide the keys to take our sport into the future.

For both of us, a key to our development as riders and horsemen was spending hundreds of hours riding on our own. In addition to working with his brothers and various trainers over the years, Peter pushed himself to excel for countless hours alone in the ring. Kim worked for lesson time, read extensively, and practiced exercises from books and clinics to hone her skills. Recognizing the importance of practicing alone, we have designed a book that can help you work on specific skills and have included a number of self-check exercises for you to try. We hope you embrace the opportunity to learn, practice, improve, and succeed!

— PETER LEONE *and* KIMBERLY S. JAUSSI, PhD

THE FUNDAMENTALS OF

Good
Riding

1 | Horse to Rider and Back Again

Without a common language, how can we communicate with our horses?

RIDING IS ALL ABOUT connecting and communicating with our horses. Why? There are two reasons: First, the feeling of relating to and riding a horse provides a sense of personal joy and develops a positive relationship with the natural world around us. That's why people say, "There's nothing as good for the inside of a man as the outside of a horse." Second, in order to achieve our goals with our horses, we need to find a way to manage the synergy that we strive to establish between ourselves (at approximately 150 pounds) and them (averaging 1,200 pounds).

So how do we do that? This chapter covers a range of topics associated with understanding, communicating with, and connecting with horses. Fundamentally, riders communicate with their horses through the effective use of the aids. The rider's position enables the aids to operate in the most effective way possible. Mutual understanding, mutual respect, and sensitivity (feeling) are necessary for a true connection to occur.

Let's Get Started!

What do we mean by "horse to rider, rider to horse?" We start off with this topic because thinking of our time with our horses in this fundamental way helps clarify the *why* of all that we do. **Why are we riding horses in the first place?** What do we hope to accomplish?

Essentially, you're trying to use your approximately 150-pound body to get your 1,200-pound horse to do what you'd like. And you want to do it in a way that allows you to truly enjoy your horse and your sport while riding safely, confidently, and correctly — and competitively, if that's your goal — and, just as important, in a way that allows the horse to truly enjoy being ridden.

Fortunately, humans have a long history of connecting with horses and training them to do what we want or need them to do. Thousands of years ago people hunted horses for food but we soon began to tame them to carry loads, pull plows, make us more effective hunters, and transport us faster and more efficiently. The use of horses for riding led to great migrations and changed the way wars were waged. Many modern equestrian sports, such as jumping, dressage, and three-day eventing, evolved from the use of horses in the military. These sports alone garner the attention and dedication of thousands of people all over the world.

Defining and considering this equine-human relationship in terms of "horse to rider, rider to horse" will help you each and every time you get on your horse. That's the overall goal — from there you can begin to identify your specific goals and the objectives or steps you need to take to achieve them.

Define Your Goals

Let's consider an example: One of your goals might be to jump a 3' 6" competition course. That's a specific goal that you can work backward from, planning steps such as buying the right horse, finding a good trainer, taking lessons, and going to progressively

---

It's a dynamic two-way relationship that results in a connection: From from horse to rider, rider to horse.

If we can't communicate, we have no chance for control over or harmony with our horses.

more challenging shows. But at the core of that goal is the fact that to compete successfully over a 3' 6" course, there must be two-way communication between you and your horse. Your aids, your position, and your relationship with your horse all *hugely* influence the quality of that connection.

To ride well, whether for pleasure or in competition, we need to understand how to communicate effectively with our horses using aids that have been tested through the centuries. To use those aids correctly, we need to have a correct position in the saddle, and just as important, we need to understand how to make friends with our horses.

Aids.
Position.
Making
friends.
The right
equipment.
These things
help us ride and
enjoy our horses.

Peter Leone on Legato at the 1996 Olympics — see appendix 3 for the whole story of the pair's long journey to make the team.

The Rider's Aids: The Buttons

As riders we communicate with our horses not by phone calls, text messages, or e-mails but through our aids.

> Each aid must be an all-star in its own right, but work with the others as a team.

THE AIDS ARE THE "buttons" riders use to make their horses go and stop. The aids allow you to power up, slow down, and turn your horse. How they function and how you use them are the basis of communication with your horse. The aids are:

- Legs
- Seat
- Hands
- Voice
- Stick and/or spurs

The primary aids are the legs and the seat. They're the ones that should always be used first to initiate and maintain everything asked of the horse.

The secondary aids are the hands, voice, and stick. They're the ones that reinforce what you are asking with your legs and seat.

In addition to these five aids, there are also the emotional aids, which are covered more thoroughly in chapter 2. While the above aids help you manage the body of the horse and help the horse understand what you're trying to do, the emotional aids help you manage the emotions, mind, and energy of the horse.

Individual Aids Working Together

Each primary and secondary aid has a particular purpose. A rider should understand how each one works independently, but always use them in coordination with the others. What does that mean?

When your aids function independently, each is attempting to fill its own particular purpose and not being used to compensate for a problem elsewhere. That means

THE BOTTOM LINE If we don't understand how our aids operate, we can't communicate with our horses.

you shouldn't have to pull on the reins for balance when you need to use your right or left leg. You can't correct a bulging shoulder with just a rein. You shouldn't have to forsake your contact, or rein length, to use your stick.

But the tricky part about individual aids is that, while they should be solid and sympathetic enough to stand on their own, they cannot be used alone. Because of the ripple effects of the aids and the fact that we use them on a living, breathing being, **no aid ever works in a vacuum**. The use of one aid always affects what the other aids do to reinforce and support that aid. And at any time the incorrect or unclear use of one aid can negate another aid, sending mixed signals to the horse without correcting the problem.

Let's Start with the Seat

Primary aids are the ones that most effectively influence the horse — the ones we should use *first*. In riding, your primary aids are the seat and the legs. We'll discuss the seat here and cover the legs in more detail in the following chapter.

The seat is the rider's single most influential aid! The effectiveness of the seat varies with the rider's posi-

tion and the rigidity or suppleness of the upper body, which enables us to manage our horse's balance and impulsion. Using your seat with your body stretched up tall while moving forward and backward allows you to help your horse shift his weight and balance. There are two main bones in the seat, and each plays a key role in giving you leverage to help your horse.

The particular horse you are riding and the movement you are executing defines how much seat you need and whether you should use one seat bone more than the other. The basis for effectively using your seat involves knowing how to shift your weight from one seat bone to another and insuring that you have equal but "kind" weight in your seat bones when necessary.

Kind weight in your seat bones suggests that your seat stays with your horse without digging or grinding. It's a seat that becomes

Know how much pressure each seat bone is putting on your horse's back.

Remember the use and nonuse of the seat. Know when to use your seat and when not to.

part of the horse's spine. It's a seat that **is sympathetic** to that spine, dripping into it like melted candle wax. A kind seat becomes one with the horse.

Let your seat work for you. Use the leverage of your seat to influence your horse and his body. Think about a horse and how its 1,200 pounds are distributed. In front of the shoulder, there's a head and a neck, about 200 pounds at best. That leaves 1,000 pounds from the shoulder back.

It makes sense to ride that part of the horse. You want to **ride the body**

Is your horse listening to your leg?

If you squeeze your leg and get no response, here is an exercise to tune up your horse's responsiveness to your leg. This exercise uses the stick to educate him to your legs.

- Sitting on your horse at the halt, bridge your reins.* Hold your stick (crop) in your free hand and allow it to rest gently behind your leg.
- Squeeze your leg and cluck, asking your horse to move immediately forward.
- If he doesn't answer, use the stick once, firmly and quickly right behind your lower leg to teach him to move forward when you close your leg. Repeat the exercise until he moves forward.
- The instant he responds, relax your leg pressure.

Repeat the exercise:

- Halt or walk.
- Squeeze and cluck.
- If no response, use the stick.

Keep practicing until your horse is moving promptly from your leg cue and you don't need the crop. This exercise uses reinforcement theory to educate your horse to move forward, or away from your leg when it's applied. An unpleasant consequence follows if your horse doesn't respond. A pleasant consequence follows if your horse does respond. Period.

*To bridge your reins, move one rein to the other hand, overlapping the reins slightly so that one hand is now holding both reins between the fingers in the traditional way.

THE CONCEPT IN ACTION: Use of the Seat | **Richard Spooner,** shown here on Cristallo, is one of the fastest and most successful riders in the world because he knows when to sit down and use his seat and when to not use his seat to provide direction to his horse and consistently ride the winning ride. It's difficult to teach someone to be a winner; either you are or you aren't, and Richard has always been a winner. His training with Hugo Simon, the great winner from Austria and rider of E.T., helped instill in Richard how to use his seat and perform out of the gallop. From California, Richard has been instrumental in raising the performance bar for West Coast riders to be fully competitive with East Coast riders. Richard, along with fellow West Coast riders Will and Nicki Simpson and Rich Fellers, can win anywhere in the world on any given day.

Stick and spur.
Crayon and
fine pencil.
Have them both.
Know how to
use them.

of the horse. To effectively manage those thousand pounds, you need your most powerful aid, your seat. Your seat can help you create energy (impulsion) in the hindquarters and channel it forward through your legs to your hands so your horse uses himself correctly and in balance.

The Use and Nonuse of the Seat

The seat is the most influential aid because it can provide so much leverage. When a rider sits in the saddle, it's called a **three-point seat** because there are three points of contact with the horse: the two legs and the seat. The three-point position allows riders to use their seats to effectively communicate with their horses.

But as important as using the seat is the ability to not use it. Not using the seat involves knowing how to put the seat into neutral to eliminate its influence. One very effective way to not use your seat is to ride in **two-point position or half-seat**, in which you close your hip angle and stretch up in your stirrups to get up off your seat. This leaves just two points of contact with the horse — your legs.

The two-point is also called the *forward seat* and *riding with the motion*. As jumping riders we spend a significant amount of time in this position. While a fluid and sympathetic seat, it can also leave the rider in a vulnerable and weak position.

What's the advantage of the two-point seat? The nonuse of the seat may be the right tactic when your horse is objecting to your seat during times of stress or discomfort.

Two Secondary Aids: The Stick, the Spur, or Both?

Need some fine shading in your artwork? Through the ages riders have used a stick or crop, spurs, or both as reinforcements for their legs. Called the **artificial aids**, these are in the toolbox of nearly all riders. It is important to understand how to select and use the stick and/or

The Gas Pedal

Just like a car should move forward when you touch the gas pedal, your horse should move forward when you apply leg. If the gas pedal in your car isn't responding, you take it to the mechanic for fixing rather than continuing to stomp on it and hoping your car will respond. Your stick and spur can help recalibrate your horse's reaction to your leg aid, just as a mechanic can recalibrate your gas pedal!

the spur effectively to accomplish the job at hand.

It's like using a crayon to draw a picture, as opposed to a fine pencil. While you can do some art with a crayon, you can include much more detail, more sophistication, more shading with a fine pencil.

The stick is used to educate the horse to the leg or to discipline the horse. It's the crayon — use it for the broad idea and general education. It's the rider's job to make sure that the education is crystal clear and sharp. That means if you apply your leg and the horse doesn't respond (and you're sure that "noise" from your position and other aids isn't canceling out the request of your leg), you should use the stick.

Use spurs to sophisticate your ride. Once you have control of your legs and can consistently apply them in a careful, purposeful way, spurs can be used to help soften the horse's body and increase his responsiveness to the leg. Spurs enable the leg to be stronger, but they also serve as a fine pencil, giving the leg "shading" and nuance that can add sophistication to your horse's training and your ride. While you can do some art with a crayon (the stick), you can include much more detail, more sophistication, more shading with a fine pencil (the spur).

Use Your Stick Successfully

The keys to using your crop successfully are timing, consistency, and skill.

TIMING. Use the crop promptly to correct a lack of response to the leg. Otherwise, your horse won't make any connection between your action and his reaction.

CONSISTENCY. Use the stick consistently as clear reinforcement so your horse won't be confused. That way, he will learn the correct response to your leg.

SKILL. If you become disorganized and can't deliver an effective reminder, your horse may trot off as he pleases without learning anything at all except that he was just smacked for no apparent reason.

Ride the Body: the 1,000 pounds from the shoulder back, not the 200 pounds from the shoulder forward.

Thinking about Position: Form and Function

Good form enables good function. Good position allows the aids to be effective, which enables good function.

> The **most important** thing about position **is not that it looks good** – it's what it lets you do.

How is position different from the aids? Your position is where the parts of your body are when you're sitting on a horse. Your aids are what you do with your body parts. Correct position allows your aids to function effectively to direct your horse.

In order to use your aids effectively and ask your horse to do what you'd like, you *must* consider your position — where your legs, seat, body, arms, and head are supposed to be.

Here's a quick rundown of an effective position:

- **LEGS:** Heels down. Stirrups on the balls of your feet. Stirrup irons hit your ankle bones when feet are out of the stirrups.

- **SEAT:** Seat toward the front, in the "twist," or narrowest part of the saddle. Equal weight on each seat bone.

- **BODY:** A straight line from your ear to your shoulder to your hip to your heel. Core muscles relaxed but solidly set without collapsing.

- **ARMS:** Elbows bent and relaxed; arms elastic, like wet rope. Arms make a straight line from your elbow to the horse's mouth. A solid wrist (not broken), with thumbs at a 45-degree angle. Three fingers closed around the reins, with the thumb and forefinger anchoring the reins.

- **HEAD:** Head up and eyes looking toward your destination.

THE BOTTOM LINE Understanding the elements of correct position helps you clearly use your aids for optimal communication with your horse.

About that last point, a wise old cowboy named Don Swan once said, "What are you lookin' at? Lookin' for money? Lookin' to see if your horse is still there? You'll be the first one to know if your horse isn't there!"

The Two-Point Position Helps the Lines

As jumping riders we spend a great deal of time in the two-point. But we probably need to spend more. Riding in two-point can significantly help strengthen your position. When in two-point, your hip should still be over your leg. That straight line never, ever changes. It's the angle in your upper body that changes a bit in order to bring your seat slightly out of the saddle. Your hips close slightly, and your shoulders move a bit more forward relative to your hip.

The key is that **the angle in your knee should never change.** Your leg should stay the same, regardless of whether you're in two-point or three-point. Your anchor of support and balance is your steady lower leg and deep heel!

spotcheck

How's Your Position?

Even though we have all been told about position over and over again, and have some sense of where we're supposed to have our bodies, we need to check frequently and see that everything is in the right spot. Here are some quick ways to do that:

1. Have a friend take a picture of you riding from the side, at the halt, the walk, the trot, and the canter. **Can you draw a straight line** from your ear to your shoulder to your hip to your heel?

2. Without a camera-toting friend around, the easiest way to check if your leg is underneath your hip is to sit on your horse at the halt, with your head facing straight ahead. Now glance down without moving your head. **Can you see the toe of your boot?** If so, your leg is too far out in front — open up your hip and draw your whole leg back until you cannot see the toe.

3. Here's another test: Have someone stand in front of you. **Can they see the sole of your heel?** If your heels are down far enough, they should be able to see the sole of your heel, not just the sole of your toe.

Heels Down!

Always keep your heels down. When you know what to do, put your weight in your heels. When you don't know what to do, put your weight in your heels! Keeping your weight in your heels anchors your balance and gives you strength on a horse.

Three-Point to Two-Point

Check your
position at
the start of
your ride
and every few
minutes during
your ride. Today.
Every day.

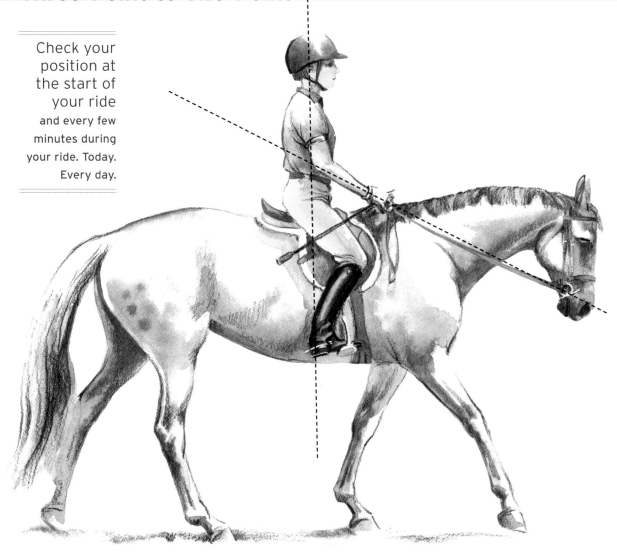

Note two key straight lines — one from the rider's ear to her shoulder to her
hip to her ankle and the other from her elbow to the horse's mouth.

Great
position is
a habit (work
on forming
yours today!).

When you move from the three-point to the two-point, your hip angle changes as your lower leg moves slightly under you to support your new upper-body position with "no seat."

How's Your Two-Point?

Here's a good exercise to practice daily.

- Get up in your two-point at the walk.

- Pick up a trot.

- Trot 10 steps, then halt.

- Return to the trot.

- Trot while making regular changes of direction for 90 seconds.

Repeat the exercise a number of times, keeping your balance stable throughout your transitions and changes of direction.

The two-point also helps you find the truth about how your seat is affecting your horse – whether your seat is driving him forward or actually inhibiting him by acting as a stiff emergency brake that's always on.

How does the two-point help you know this? To answer this question try this:

- Step into the canter while in a three-point seat.

- Immediately go into a two-point seat.

- Watch what happens.

Your horse will either go softer and slower than normal, or faster and stronger than normal, or he will canter exactly the same. **If he slows down,** that means your seat is doing some driving while you're sitting on it. **If he speeds up,** it means your seat is resisting or inhibiting his movement. **If his canter remains the same,** then he is balanced and accomplishing the goal of accepting the aids and carrying himself.

Also notice how your horse's expression changes; if his ears were back but go forward when you go up, then perhaps your seat was making him less than happy. And pay attention to whether your hand and reins pull when you're seated but give when you're in three-point.

THE CONCEPT IN ACTION: Good Form Enables Good Function | Two-time Olympic Gold Medalist (2004 and 2008) **McLain Ward** is the master of a perfect position. No matter which horse, which show, which class, McLain always keeps the line from his heel to his hip to his shoulder in textbook position as he gallops around the course. His position over the jump is equally impeccable: deep heel, perfect lower leg position, centered and balanced upper body. His excellent position enables excellent connection and influence with his mounts, balance, focus, and power to consistently make clean jumping efforts over the largest and most technical courses. McLain may well be the best rider of our time with his mastery of position, his insatiable commitment to winning, and his total dedication to understanding the key details of the sport. Here McLain is riding his two-time Team Gold Medal mount, Sapphire, in Wellington, Florida.

THE CONCEPT IN ACTION: Make Friends with Your Horse | One of our sport's best examples of a great horse/rider relationship was **Eric Lamaze** and the sensational **Hickstead**. Hickstead, pictured above, was a small, complex, and high-energy horse that many of the world's top riders passed up. Eric's uncanny ability to understand and sense what Hickstead needed and what he was capable of resulted in arguably the most successful combination in the show-jumping world. With its blend of feeling, mechanics, and talent, they produced a list of international wins that is among the longest in the history of our sport. It includes the Grand Prix of Aachen, the Spruce Meadows Masters, and an individual Gold Medal at the 2008 Beijing Olympic Games. Individually, Eric and Hickstead were extremely gifted athletes but it was their chemistry together, their BFF relationship that made them the best in the world.

Make Friends with Your Horse

Build the relationship.

WHEN WAS THE LAST TIME you *invited* your horse to do something? Gave him the opportunity to work for you? Made friends with him in the midst of a difficult transition or exercise?

Making friends with your horse takes **a different kind of mind-set**. It means introducing him to an exercise or job with respect. It's about making sure he trusts you as a friend and has confidence in what you are asking of him.

What do we mean by "have a relationship with your horse"? Well, all the aids in the world might result in a horse's doing what you demand out of fear, but that is not riding! That is not having an understanding and connection with your horse; that is not a relationship. When you do have that connection, those same aids will result in your horse responding out of respect and commitment. The difference is substantial in your and your horse's performance, competitiveness, and enjoyment!

This different kind of mind-set starts with respect for the horse and interacting with sensitivity and feeling. Open your senses to **identify the physical, mental, and emotional states of your horse** and then use your aids to guide, manage, and correct your mount accordingly.

We know how to "friend" people on Facebook, but how do we "friend" our mounts?

Look for opportunities to make friends with your horse, but more importantly, treat him as you would a friend – with respect, compassion, and boundaries.

THE BOTTOM LINE Building a relationship with your horse increases the effectiveness of your two-way communication.

Develop a relationship with your horse.

Earn his trust.
Make friends
with him.

Making friends starts with respect for the horse and interacting with sensitivity and feeling. Rewarding your horse is an essential part of the process. It's as simple as a soft stroke or scratch after a transition well done. Relaxing your fingers, decreasing the intensity of your leg pressure, or exhaling deeply all serve as rewards to your horse after he does something correctly.

Your horse is not a tool you put back in the garage when you're done with your ride. Horses who like their jobs and trust their riders perform better. It's your job to give your horse confidence in your program. The way you ride shows your horse that you appreciate him. Working together and having a connection results in both of you reaching a "good place" and feeling confident in your relationship.

Reinforce and Stimulate

Horses like routine and find comfort in repetition. It is our job to establish a routine and at the same time make the daily ride interesting to our horses. Always try to reinforce with routine and stimulate with the unexpected. Each ride should combine a mixture of expected daily exercises with unexpected questions. The magical result is that the horse not only masters the expected but also looks for and answers the unexpected questions.

The Importance of the Right Equipment

Less is more: Choose equipment carefully and make sure you aren't looking for a quick fix to a complicated problem.

AN IMPORTANT ASPECT of riding is the tack and equipment and all that "stuff" that helps us communicate with our horses. Or *not*! Often our choice of tack and equipment actually garbles communication with our mounts and makes the connection fuzzy and filled with static. It's important to understand how **tack and equipment can help or hinder** the communication and connection with our horses.

We believe that "less is better" — that clear, crisp communication is grounded in classical horsemanship, not a pile of straps and buckles. Some pieces of tack do help us, though, so choose carefully. You should always have the tools that are most appropriate for your horse and the job at hand.

Have to Have the Latest Stuff?

Everyone likes cool stuff and cool horse stuff is better yet. The latest boots, the hottest tack, whatever the top riders are using — only the best for your horse, right? Not necessarily. Things that are "in" may not give you a leg up on the competition and might actually hinder your performance. **We're not saying you can't have cool stuff, but know why you have it!** Before you buy a new piece of equipment or change bits, think about if it's absolutely necessary to fix a particular problem and about possible negative impacts.

Chances are you've longed for and perhaps even saved up to buy something like the latest pair of back boots. They're hard to resist, offering

When it comes to equipment, less is often more.

THE BOTTOM LINE The right equipment can help you ride better, but only if you choose, and use, it properly.

support, protection, and cushioning, and they make our horse look sharp. Having the hottest equipment makes us feel like top athletes on top horses who should be taken more seriously. But the wrong boots on the wrong horse can actually *hurt* your performance.

The simpler, the better.

It's the same with your bit. You may *think* you want a bit that everyone else is using, such as a three-ring snaffle or a Pelham. But your horse may actually go best in a simple D-ring snaffle. Use the bit that is the *least* your horse needs. If you need more, you can move up from there. Don't use the bit that everyone else is using. Find the bit that is just right for you and your horse.

Can You Ride Your Horse without It?

Most problems are solved through good riding, not equipment. Always look first to how you are riding (Too much hand? Not enough leg? Inconsistent aids?) before trying a new piece of equipment. Make sure your horse is sound enough and properly conditioned for the job you're asking him to do. And don't forget to check that he fully understands what you want him to do — he may not be resisting, just confused!

Always ask if a new piece of equipment is the appropriate tool for the job at hand or if you're just dressing up your horse in what is cool. When considering tack and equipment, ask yourself these questions:

- What is the least I need to get the job done?

- What are my options for the job at hand?

- How might it help my riding and my horse's performance?

- How might it hurt my riding and my horse's performance?

Go through your tack and accessories and ask yourself why you're using each piece. Is it something that you're *certain* is the least you can do with? For example, if you're using a full cheek snaffle with a slow twist, are you sure your horse won't go well in a lesser bit? Periodically explore using less bit, starting at home where the surroundings and routine are familiar.

Carefully consider everything you use, and if you're not certain, see if you can do without it. Have a clear reason to use the tack you're using. Know its purpose and be aware of the potential problems it can cause.

One piece of tack that is often used incorrectly is draw reins. People often use them to "get a horse's head down" or to "set a horse's head." There isn't a more incorrect reason than that for using draw reins. Draw reins should be used only under the supervision of professionals with a strong understanding of how to drive the horse correctly from back to front, with the draw reins used in conjunction with the legs and seat to engage the horse's hind end or for additional control.

Here you can see from the looseness in the draw rein that the horse's head is not being forced down with the draw reins. He is round from behind, with his hind end engaged and his back lifting up to allow him to move forward into the contact of the snaffle rein.

Laura Kraut
on Cedric at
the Wellington
Winter Equestrian
Festival, 2007

2 | The Biggest Keys

Success in riding comes from riding the whole horse, riding the body of the horse from back to front, and riding with your legs, not your hands. Always.

THERE ARE **three big keys** for effective riding and for success with your horse in equestrian sports. No matter which sport you consider or ride in, these keys remain the same:

- Ride the *whole* horse, emotions and all, not just part of the horse.

- Ride the horse from back to front; don't just steer the front end. The engine is in the back.

- Ride with your legs and seat in conjunction with your hands to create and manage the energy of the whole horse.

In chapter 1 we talked about the aids and how you must consider them as an integrated set of "buttons" with which you tell your horse what to do. In this chapter we explain *why* you must not consider the aids as separate, completely independent buttons. They're not.

When you're on your horse, each aid you use is influenced to some degree by the other aids, your position on the horse, and by the whole horse itself. That whole horse is wrapped up inside its emotional state and in yours. That's why it's important to ride the whole horse (mentally and emotionally) while also focusing on riding the body from back to front with your legs, not your hands.

The Whole Horse: Mind and Body

A rigid horse is not a rideable horse.
A relaxed horse is a rideable horse.

In riding the whole horse, you must ride **with your whole self.**

IT'S NATURAL, when you ride, to think mostly about riding the physical horse that you're sitting on. You see his neck in front of you, you touch his sides with your legs, you make him move under you. And as you ride you tend to focus on the "aid of the moment," using the one that is necessary for what you're asking of the horse at that point in time. So you tend to think in parts — more leg, more hand, haunches out, head up or down. **Stop thinking in parts!**

To be a successful rider, you need to think about riding the *whole* horse each and every time you get on. It's a philosophical thing as well as a physics thing. There is absolutely no part of a horse that is disconnected or independent of any other part of it. To ride on part of a horse is to ride all of it.

Remember the Emotional Aids

These are the aids you use as a rider to help manage your horse's emotional state. A "ride the whole horse" philosophy requires that you manage the emotions of your horse, that you help your horse to relax *and* work. When a horse can relax while he's working, the result is a soft horse that has self-carriage. Without relaxation you have nothing. A relaxed horse is a softer, more willing, naturally more supple horse. **A relaxed horse accepts the rider and her aids, setting the stage for the ultimate partnership.**

THE BOTTOM LINE Consider both the mind and body of your horse, and know that a relaxed horse is a softer, more compliant, and more rideable horse.

What exactly do we mean by the emotional aids? **How do we manage the emotions of the horse?** As we discussed in chapter 1, building a relationship — making friends with your horse — goes a long way in setting the emotional stage. But what do we do when we need to calm our horse down or inspire him?

There are a variety of things you can do to manage your horse's emotions. We cover them in more detail in chapter 5, but for now let's focus on just recognizing the need to manage the emotions of your horse. How do you know if and which of your horse's emotions

need managing as you ride? Before we answer that question, you need to **realize that your emotions count, too.** In general, the rider leads by example, so that a tight, rigid rider equals a tight, rigid horse. A soft, patient rider equals a soft, patient horse.

Take stock of your own state of mind and body before riding, so that you may think about how to best manage your whole self. Ask yourself these questions:

- What's my emotional and physical state before I mount?

- Am I stressed, in pain, sad, physically weak, or overly excited about something?

- Can I bring myself to that place I know is best for my horse?

That whole self will be the one your horse will be counting on for direction, clarity, and empathy. If you're not operating as a whole — if you're not being honest about what the state of your whole being is — you'll send confusing signals that will misdirect your horse's performance that day. Within reason, we can control our physical and emotional states when we ride. The better you are at this, the more often you will have a good ride!

> A relaxed horse accepts the presence and aids of the rider. No amount of obedience in the world will compensate for a tense horse.

Start Your Ride on the Right Note

Just as you would start a workout at the gym, start your horse's outing with simple movement and stretching. You can do this by either trotting or cantering straight and forward "at the rhythm" (in a nice working gait) for three to five minutes. Once your horse's muscles are warm and he's had a chance to loosen up, you can begin your work.

THE CONCEPT IN ACTION: Riding the Emotions | **Margie Engle** knows how to create and channel the emotions of her horses. She is gifted at bringing her mounts to just the right "boil" so they are fast, without creating so much energy and fire that her horse doesn't "boil over" and bring poles down. Like the other riders highlighted in this book, Margie has always been a winner. Her ticket to the winner's circle is her gift to inspire her mounts to be the fastest they can be. In every one of her jump-offs, you can see her urging her horse forward with passion and fire – if you watch, you'll see her horse's tail up and spinning and its ears back as it races to the finish line. Here she urges Hidden Creeks Campella over a large oxer.

The Emotional Horse

Some say horses don't have emotions. We couldn't agree *less* with that statement. Horses can love or hate their jobs. They can be frightened, scared, nervous, or in pain. They can be angry, bored, irritated, frustrated, or confused. They can also be happy, joyful, excited, or playful.

Part of our job as riders is to manage the chaos for our horses — to help them process the questions we ask and to make clear what is confusing to them (whether it's from incorrect use of the aids or from noisy machinery operating near by). It's also part of our job to help them process the chaos that might be happening inside their heads.

Never forget that horses are animals that are meant to be roaming and grazing with a herd. We put them in stalls and ask them to focus on the jobs *we* want them to do. We need to recognize that and help them manage their emotional challenges. Some horses have a steady and consistent temperament and some have a constantly changing and volatile temperament.

As you would expect, a horse with a steady temperament (good character) is much easier to work with. No matter what their temperament, letting them have some downtime with their buddies or taking them out for a controlled playful gallop in the field can be helpful!

In general you can tell if your horse's emotions need managing by constantly asking yourself how he is acting and reacting. **How does he** *feel*? Looking for the signs below will help you understand your horse's emotional and physical state. Consider the following questions each time you ride:

- Are his head and ears up and focused on what is going on around him?

- Is he fresh and feeling good or is something distracting him?

- Is his back tight and tense? Is he in pain or nervous?

Learn to **manage your horse's emotions** not only from "hot" to "cool," but also from "calm" to "alert."

Read your horse.

Horses have emotions. Those **emotions can change** within any given ride and between rides.

- Is he full of energy and wanting to buck?

- Is his body hollow, with his head up?

- Is his hind end scurrying along rather than stepping forward?

- Is there white foam in his sweat (check his chest, neck, and between his hind legs), indicating nervousness?

- Does he pin his ears in distaste during transitions or when an aid is used?

- Is his step springy because he's raring to go or because he's about to panic and run?

- Is he snorting as he trots? If so, is it because he's frightened or just feeling good?

The horse is agitated and unhappy, and the rider is tense and constraining his canter. The horse's emotional needs might be better managed by the rider allowing him to relax and stretch for a few minutes before resuming work.

Ride the Body

*Always think about riding the whole body
of the horse, not just the front of the horse.*

MOST RIDERS GROW UP thinking that you turn the horse with your reins, that you halt with your hand. In classical riding, though, that is not the case. The rider does *not* turn the horse with just the reins or halt using just the hands. Not if you *ride the body*. It's a different way of thinking about riding. It takes a clear understanding of where a horse's engine is: it's in the back. **The horse is a rear-engined animal.**

For horses to execute the kinds of things asked of them as athletes, those rear engines must be operating at full capacity. You need to have your horse always moving forward across the ground, working with impulsion and carrying himself correctly.

The next time you ride, ask yourself if your horse's motor is barely

Ride the Body

Our natural inclination is to control our horses with our hands through the 5-inch bit in their mouths. That is a very small amount of horse to interact with, compared with the amount of horse our legs and seat interact with! Our legs and seat are in contact with 60 or more inches of the horse's barrel, with our entire weight sitting directly on his spine. It makes sense to use our legs and seat, which hug the body of the horse, to manage, direct, communicate with, and ride our horses.

True or false?
Your hands steer your horse.

THE BOTTOM LINE When you understand the concepts of a horse's body in motion, you can ride your horse from back to front to generate energy and power.

working because you're constantly kicking? Or is it on and purring forward with bounce and energy (self-carriage)?

That engine gives your horse the balance and ability to carry himself, to turn softly, to transition gracefully, and to answer the competitive questions you ask of him. His drive comes from the hind end. By riding your horse's body — that stuff *behind* the saddle — you help his engine generate and maintain its power.

Is the Engine Working?

Consider whether you're riding the body by having someone videotape your ride. One sign that the body is being ridden is that the horse's hind end comes up underneath him. Look closely at the video of your ride.

- Is your horse's engine running smoothly?
- Is he going forward willingly, with impulsion, without your having to constantly kick him forward?
- Is his hind end stepping up underneath his body?

The proof is in the tracks. There's no better way to learn whether you've mastered the ride-the-body key than to study your tracks in a freshly dragged arena. If you are riding the body, your horse's hind hoofprints should be either *just inside* or *in front of* his front hoofprints, not behind them or beside them. When the body is ridden, the horse can be straight.

THE CONCEPT IN ACTION: Riding the Engine | Perhaps the most successful hunter rider of our time, **Scott Stewart** is pictured above on his mount Way Cool. Scott's success comes from his ability to ride the whole horse when training and when in the showring. He rides the body of his horses from back to front, creating very soft, very correct horses that gallop brilliantly across the ground and jump in better form and style than the rest of the competition. Many think that good hunter-riding avoids using the seat and legs, but Scott's classical use of the aids and his approach to riding hunters proves otherwise. While much of U.S. Show Hunter riding has strayed from prioritizing classical schooling methods that produce horses that jump athletically with good technique, Scott provides hope for the future with his correct and classical approach to riding and winning in hunter classes all over the country.

It's All in the Legs

Steer with both legs: use them to create and maintain a chute to guide your horse.

IN CHAPTER 1 we discussed the importance of the seat, but here we focus on the legs and why they are so important. The legs do a lot: they help create power and collection (energy and speed), they manage rhythm and direction, and they act like guardrails.

Legs = Power

The legs are your gas pedal. **They create impulsion** — the rpms of the engine. They enable you to ask for animated extension and collection. Your legs create the guardrails to push your horse through. Along with the seat, they are the power buttons.

Legs = Rhythm

You can use your legs to reinforce the rhythm of a gait; you can also use them to ask for and support different gaits, or a different rhythm within a gait. For example, when you post the two-beat trot, you activate your horse's hind end with your legs each time you post. With a canter you keep a more constant pressure through the three beats of the gait. Using your legs and your seat together enables you to manage your horse's rhythm, stride length, and impulsion.

Legs = Collection

The legs are also collection buttons. You use them to ride your horse into collection, whether it be at the walk, trot, or canter. Use your legs to create more energy from behind (impulsion). Collecting your horse requires a great deal of leg — often times more than extension does.

THE BOTTOM LINE Your legs are critically important aids that initiate and maintain extension and collection, establish rhythm, and bend and straighten your horse's body.

How Are Your Legs Working?

To practice riding the body of the horse with your legs instead of with your hands, hook your thumbs together while walking your horse. Choose a point in the arena to turn your horse off the rail, using just your legs. Your outside leg will help the body of the horse begin and complete the turn.

Note how much you wish you could use your hands: it's a telltale sign of how much you have (or haven't) been using your legs to ride the body!

ARE YOU APPLYING THE BIGGEST KEYS? One way to see if you're mastering the biggest keys is to practice going from an extended canter to a collected canter without breaking to the trot — on a circle. Try this:

- Place two cones opposite one another on a 60-foot (18 m) circle.
- At one cone extend the canter.
- When you reach the other cone, stretch up, squeeze hard, and collect the canter.

At a typical canter with a 12-foot (3.5 m) stride, this size circle should take approximately 16 strides — try to get 15 strides on the extended part and 19 strides on the collected part.

Throughout this exercise, watch your horse's emotions. Ask yourself the questions on pages 33 and 34. Consider these also:

- Is your horse's body staying on the arc of the circle as you do this exercise?
- Are you riding the horse from his back end to front end?
- Is he falling in or bulging out of the circle?
- When you ask your horse to extend or collect, how quickly and correctly does he respond?
- Finally, are your legs working harder for the collection than your hands? (They should be!)

If you can successfully complete this exercise, congratulations — you're well on your way to mastering the biggest keys!

Legs = Steering Wheels

You turn the horse with both legs in conjunction with both reins. It's a tricky concept, especially if you've initially been taught to turn only with your hands. But in classical riding, your horse moves away from your leg. When asking your horse to turn left, use your right leg. That's one piece of it.

The other piece of turning with your leg is that **the turn is an exercise in riding forward**. To change direction, a horse must use his hind end to drive his body through the turn. Much like a car in a turn, the horse's engine must be activated for him to come out of a turn without losing balance or impulsion. In a turn, just as in collection, the horse's springs must be loaded for a successful execution.

Legs = Guardrails

Finally, the legs act as guardrails. They play a vital role in guiding your horse to travel straight across the ground. With every step, your legs create a chute and your seat pushes the body of the horse through this chute.

Your legs also **bend your horse**, with the inside leg pushing the horse into the outside one. If your horse isn't bending or isn't traveling straight, then you're not using your legs properly in conjunction with your other aids.

Your legs are the guardrails. Use them.

THE CONCEPT IN ACTION: It's All in the Legs | Nowhere do you need your legs more than in Grand Prix jumping, because the winning ride will be a masterpiece of "go" and "turn." Next to strategy the legs play the key role. **Georgina Bloomberg** understands this. Here she is turning her horse, Curius, right with her left leg and left rein against the outside of the horse in the air over this large oxer. She is using her eyes to initiate and cue the rest of her aids to support the turn.

Elizabeth Pandich
on Limited Edition
at Lionshare
Farm, Greenwich,
Connecticut

3 Focus on the Flat

Ride every day knowing that the better your quality of flatwork, the better your performance will be in all disciplines of the sport.

FLATWORK, FLATTING, DRESSAGE, HACKING: It doesn't matter what you call it. **Flatwork** is all about training and developing your horse *without* jumping. Working on the flat through a variety of exercises makes him forward, soft, supple, and straight. When you understand the importance of flatwork in relation to jumping, you can develop concrete goals for developing your horse and your riding and know when you're ready for each step.

In this chapter we look at what to think about when doing flatwork. The material in chapter 2 is a backdrop for everything we cover here. As we utilize the biggest keys, this chapter outlines four additional points to focus on as you work your horse on the flat:

- **GOALS** – what you want to achieve in your riding

- **CONTACT** – maintaining your connection with your horse

- **TRANSITIONS** – changing between gaits and within gaits

- **"YOU'RE READY WHEN"** – knowing when to take the next steps of your ride

> The better the quality of your flatwork, **the better the quality of your jumping performance.**

Why focus on the flat? Because flatwork does it all. Flatwork is where you create all the connections you need for everything else you do with your horse, be it jumping in an arena or foxhunting in a field. Through a solid grounding in flatwork, you help your horse to become soft, obedient, fluid, supple, and educated to your aids. You also help him develop strength, balance, and precision, so he can carry a rider and do his job in balance and with focus.

Two-time Olympic Team Silver Medalist Anne Kursinski is a perfect example of a master of flatwork whose preparation enables her to be a master over jumps. Her focus on flatwork in her training program gives her the precision she needs to excel at the championship level. Here her mount is Roxanna.

Setting Goals

*Focusing on specific goals motivates your
riding and helps your horse go better.*

TARGETS AND GOALS help people be better riders. How? Without going too deeply into psychology research, **having a specific but difficult goal helps you be more motivated** and guides your training efforts as you make progress. It gives your brain something to focus on. The specificity of the goal helps you understand it and directs your day-to-day riding. The "stretch" toward a difficult (but attainable) goal is the only way to improve yourself and your horse.

Okay, goals help people focus. Great. But what does that have to do with flatwork? It's like this: Many riders set goals for their horses and riding, for the season or even the whole year, perhaps something like, "We'll move up to the 3' divisions this year." We discuss creating those larger goals for your show season and riding career in chapter 10, but for now let's focus on translating that bigger goal into day-to-day actions and rides. **And that boils down to flatwork.**

It's not often that the average rider says "Well, if my goal is to move up to the 3' divisions this year, what does that mean for my flatwork today?" Rather (and unfortunately), it's more likely to be, "Wednesdays, Fridays, and Sundays are my jumping days. Tuesday is a flatting day, so I'll just hack."

If you think like that, *stop it!* Your goals for your flatwork translate directly into successes in your work over fences. Proper flatwork gives you the balance, timing, and precision you need over fences.

> Flatwork
> does it all.
> Don't think of
> it as jumping;
> think of it as
> an extension
> of flatwork.

THE BOTTOM LINE Setting goals in your daily riding repertoire helps your flatwork, your focus, and your rate of progress in training your horse.

THE CONCEPT IN ACTION: Setting Goals | Ten-time Olympian **Ian Millar** is a master of the show ring because he is the best at setting long-term, intermediate, and short-term goals and relating them to his daily, monthly, and annual training. A winner from day one, Ian combines his talent in the saddle with the insight of an intelligent horseman who studies the details: how a horse performs, thinks, learns; what is being asked by a course designer in order to jump a clear round; what striding and track are needed to win; and what sequence of experiences a horse needs to have to be ready to peak at a given Championship. This means giving thought to the long-term training experience for your horse and breaking it down from the overall plan for the year to what you work on in a given day. One of my favorite "Ian-isms" is, "Show me a good loser and you've shown me a real loser." Here Ian demonstrates international style and position on up-and-coming star Dryden.

Jumping Is Flatwork with Airborne Moments

The same fundamentals are at work in both flatwork and jumping: Straightness, balance, softness, effective communication, rhythm, and timing. That's because jumping is flatwork with airborne moments. So focus on your flatwork, and set specific goals for you and your horse. It will help your jumping! Goals help improve performance when they are:

- Specific
- Difficult but achievable
- Meaningful

Let's break that down for flatwork.

Specific

A specific goal can be measured and tracked. An example on the flat might be "to soften the left side of my horse's mouth and body." To achieve a given goal, you draw upon your knowledge and experience to do exercises that address the problem. In this case, a number of patiently done leg yields, changes of direction, and transitions would help you meet your goal.

Difficult but Achievable

Are properly executed changes of direction difficult for you and your horse? It may be hard to change

your bend and maintain a regular rhythm or pace. It may take a lot of concentration to keep that pace and also commit to the correct track of your exercise. In that case, this exercise may indeed fit the "difficult but attainable" criterion for good goal setting.

But those changes of direction may be too easy. Or too hard. Neither case is good for goal-setting because when the work is too easy or too hard, you won't maximize the learning or training curve. If you find that an exercise is too easy, make it harder. In the case of a serpentine, that might mean doing five-loop serpentines instead of three-loop ones. If you find that an exercise is too difficult, try breaking it down into smaller pieces. If a five-loop serpentine is too hard, try three loops.

Meaningful

The final part of setting goals is to make sure they mean something to your riding. Hopefully, the meaningful part is covered simply because you care about your riding and want to improve. But your goals may be more meaningful than that. Consider that "Move up to the 3' divisions" goal.

Wanting to move up a division makes a goal of "riding twice a week

Developing goals directs your flatwork — **better flatwork** means **better jumping!**

Always conservatively **"push the envelope"** of what you and your horse are working on.

without stirrups" more meaningful, because if you lose your stirrup
over a bigger fence in the show ring,
you're more vulnerable. But if your
goals have included work without
stirrups on the flat, your balance is
better, and you are a stronger rider.
You'll be more competitive in the
bigger division.

Setting Specific Goals

Your goals for a day of flatwork
might include a list like this:

- 14 upward transitions

- 14 downward transitions

- 7 serpentines

- 8 leg yields (4 each
  direction)

- Staying 4 feet off the rail

- 5 half turns in reverse

- 5 center lines

- 7 halts

As you can imagine, starting
a ride off with goals such
as these very much changes
the type of ride you'll have.
It will be a more focused,
more productive ride that
will improve your straightness, your balance, and your
horse's obedience and
balance — in short, your
connection.

If you write your specific
goals down, you'll be able to
look back and notice that
while your goals help your
performance, they don't
focus on your position at all.
It is important to constantly
remind yourself to police
your position, as you will
only improve your horse on
the flat if your technique
(using the aids from the
correct position) is correct.
So you might add a goal
that helps your position
improve, such as:

- 10 minutes in two-point
  three times a week

Contact:
Tying It All Together

Contact completes the connection from the rider to the horse and back again.

IMAGINE THIS SCENARIO: You're having a lesson or perhaps warming up for a class. You hear your trainer say, "Soften your hand." "Relax your hand." "Let go of your horse's face." "Stop pulling!" "Let your arm follow." "Relax your arms" "Your hand is too stiff."

Then you hear, "Shorten your reins." "Package your horse." "Take a feel." "Give your horse something to trot into." "His head is all over the place." "Your reins are flopping!"

You might be thinking, "*Aargh!* Why is he saying one thing, then another? I wish he'd just tell me what to do and quit changing his mind."

Longitudinal Exercise

Contact can help package a horse's energy that is coming from behind — something we call "longitudinal" because it's from back to front. Anything that involves shortening and lengthening your horse is longitudinal in nature. Collections, extensions, moving up, and waiting are all longitudinal exercises and require that your body, hands, seat, and legs work together to maintain the back-to-front connection in all your movements.

Contact is not about yanking, sawing, or flopping. Contact is a kind, empathetic feeling that communicates.

THE BOTTOM LINE Classical riding is not about pulling on the reins but about pushing the horse with your legs into the contact so you can connect with the whole horse.

Contact
completes the
connection:
ride with
sympathy,
compassion, and
feeling in
your hands.

Weak
hands=
absent or
intermittent
communication
with your horse.

But he's not changing his mind — he's talking the whole time about **contact**. He's talking about developing a gentle, consistent communication with your horse's mouth. He's talking about harnessing the impulsion you create from the horse's rear engine. But what does that look like? What does that feel like?

It's Like Playing a Guitar

Consider a guitar. For the instrument to make its best sound — for the energy to come up through the string — there has to be an ideal amount of tension in the string. If it's too loose, the sound is wobbly or squishy. If it's too tight, it pings or whines.

Your reins are similar. Your hand conducts the energy that your leg produces. To capture the energy

and package the "sound" or connection, you have to invite your horse to move into the contact. His energy, or impulsion, has to have somewhere to go for the connection to be complete. Your contact with your horse enables you to establish a consistent connection with the whole horse.

Consider this: If you were riding at a walk and a friend walked up to your horse and plucked your reins the way you'd pluck a guitar or violin string, what would your friend sense? Would the string (rein) be too taut — as though if it were made out of something other than thick leather it would break? If so, there's too much weight in your hand. Would the string (rein) flop? Then there's not enough of a feel between you and the horse's mouth.

spotcheck

Can You Do a Two-Finger Canter?

During a workout, pick up a canter. When your horse feels focused and engaged, try to hold your reins with just your thumb and your forefinger. Keep cantering. **What happens?**

If your horse is truly connected through your contact, he will be so light that it's perfectly possible to canter with just two fingers. If your contact is too heavy, then two fingers won't be able to hold it. Your horse will lose his frame and balance because he's been depending on your heavy hand.

Being able to have your horse round and going on the bit with only two fingers on the reins means that your legs and seat are maintaining his shape and the connection between you. It means your horse is carrying himself. Congratulations – self-carriage is a stretch goal!

The Circle of Aids

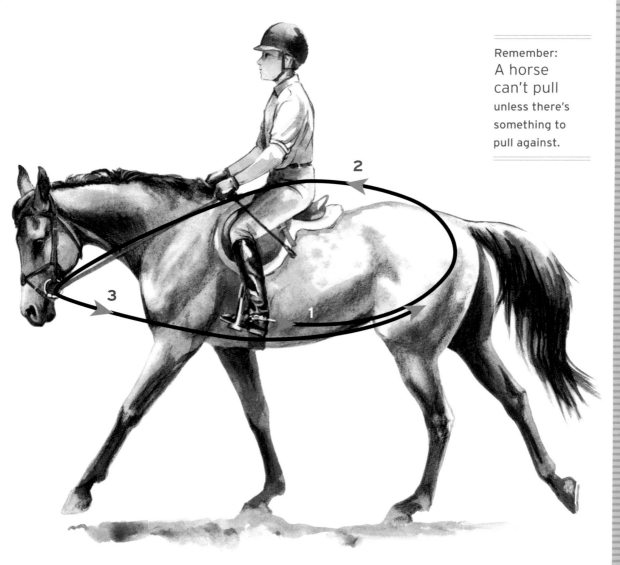

Remember:
A horse can't pull
unless there's something to pull against.

Correct and consistent contact results from a recurring circle of connection, as shown above. While this horse and rider do not fully demonstrate the correct engagement of the hind end, they do show the movement of energy.

The key parts of this ongoing circle are
1) the rider's legs and seat engage the horse's hind end
2) the rider engages the back (topline) from back to front and
3) the rider supports the use of the hind end and topline to create a soft mouth, resulting in a light front end.

Are You Feeling the Contact?

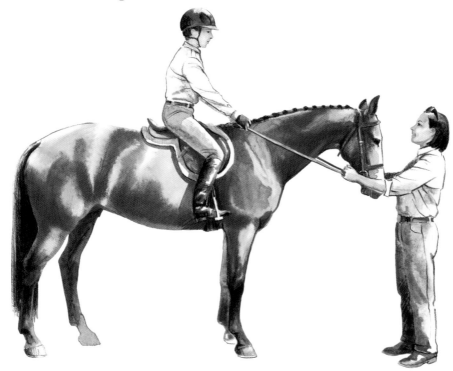

Put yourself in your horse's place. How does contact feel to him? Try this:

- Have a friend sit on her horse. Stand in front of the horse, facing the rider.

- Put one hand on each rein, just behind the bit. You are now the horse's mouth.

WHAT DO YOU FEEL?
- Ask your friend to add another pound of resistance.

WHAT DOES THAT FEEL LIKE?
- Ask your friend to soften. Do the reins flop?

WHAT WOULD THOSE FLOPPY REINS FEEL LIKE AT THE TROT?

- Now "turn" right, then left. Use slight pressure and see if your rider's hand follows.

DOES THE WEIGHT IN EACH REIN CHANGE?

Imagine how your horse feels while marching around the ring as you ride different shapes. It's difficult to keep a constant feel of your horse's mouth through all shapes and transitions and at all the gaits. It takes a lot of practice to get that feel right and to be consistent.

Contact Is a Conversation

Contact is a respectful, kind feel of your horse's mouth — no pulling or flopping. If you keep taking, pulling, and sawing, you'll create a heavy horse that resents your hand. **The contact must be sensitive and respectful.** With taking must come soft giving: reward by relaxing your fingers. It's a conversation, an invisible one that the horse will understand.

If you have a heavy hand, you'll create a heavy horse that pulls on the reins and ignores your aids. Similarly, if you ride with a weak hand, or a hand that isn't communicating consistently with the horse, you won't have any relationship with the horse and his movements.

Broken wrists are the number-one culprit of weak hands, because the line from the horse's mouth to the rider's elbow is disjointed. It creates static in the conversation, so the horse cannot hear what you're trying to tell him.

The Recipe for Good Contact

To create good contact you need the following ingredients:

Impulsion. The right kind of energy, produced from behind and coming up into the horse's front end.

Closed legs. You need to close your legs to feel your horse's mouth. Push the horse to get the right amount of resistance.

Short reins. It's very difficult for your reins to be too short. But they can be too long (and often are). How do you know if your reins are the right length? Your hands should sit approximately 4 to 6 inches (10 to 15 cm) in front of your pommel.

Closed fingers. Without closed fingers, your reins will slide out of your hand and your length will need constant readjustment.

> **Connection between horse and rider** allows harmony, empathy, and the ability to work toward a common goal.

It's a Cycle

The energy moves from your leg through your horse's body and connects through the contact to the horse's mouth. Contact is about the connection with the legs and the seat and the influence of your back on your horse's body, which then goes through your arms, through your hands to your horse's mouth, and back through his body.

Solid wrists. Flat or broken wrists weaken the connection. It should feel as though your forearm bone goes right into your hands.

Full body connection. Contact starts from your upper torso, with a connected, stretched upper back and square shoulders. Those two foundations allow your arms to hang and your elbows to create about a 95-degree angle.

Take these ingredients and ride your horse into a light, balanced connection. The result is a horse that is moving forward with impulsion, on its own accord, into a kind, consistent feel. That's good contact.

From the elbow you don't want anything weakening the relationship with the horse's mouth. You want the energy from behind that's coming up through the horse's back and spine into the front end to be harnessed, packaged, wrapped in a light but constant feel, as shown on the top. The "broken wrist" shown by the rider on the bottom results in a weak and inconsistent contact.

Steffen Peters, shown here riding Weltino's Magic, demonstrates the position, connection, and performance that make it easy to understand why he's one of the best riders in the world. No matter what the discipline, correct contact is essential. Note his perfect upper-body position and balance. A straight line runs from his elbow to his horse's mouth and his hands are an extension of his forearms, with his thumbs at a 45°-angle and his fingers closed on the reins. His eyes are the beginning and ending of his exceptional balance and concentration.

try this

Pick up a dressage whip or a longe whip, something on the longer side, not a short jumping bat. **Put the popper end of the whip into a wall, with the whip parallel to the floor. Stand at the end of the whip, and push. What happens? The whip lifts up in the center.**

Well, think of the whip as your horse. **The butt of the whip is your horse's hind end. The wall provides the constant feel, like correct contact does. Your push is your leg, producing energy to change the shape of the whip. And the middle lifts up, just as your horse's back lifts when he is moving forward into a contact.**

Now hold the whip in front of you with one hand around the butt end and one hand on the other end. **Again, the butt end is the hind end, and the other is the head. Practice holding with your "head" hand and driving/pushing with your "hind" hand. Keep playing with the two concepts – driving and offering the appropriate contact – until your "horse" is "round" with its "back" lifted.**

Transitions: Change It Up

Transitions help put a mouth on a horse.

NO DAY ON A HORSE is ever exactly the same as the one before or the ones to come. That's part of the beauty of riding: It's challenging and exciting. It keeps us on our toes and always requires that we stay on top of our game.

Just as change is part of riding horses overall, it is also part of each individual ride. **Making transitions should be a part of every ride.** Ask for transitions within and between gaits. Ask your horse to change bends, to change direction, to change frames, to change energy, to change paces. Make your flatwork training interesting for your horse by regularly changing from one question to another in a timely manner.

How do transitions improve your horse and your riding? In a nutshell, transitions help you develop:

- Balance
- Accuracy
- Timing
- Obedience
- Impulsion
- Suppleness

You can do transitions between gaits and within the walk, trot, and canter. You do transitions within a gait in the form of extension and collection.

When we talk about transitions *between* gaits, we're talking about asking your horse to go from one gait to another, say, from walk to trot. Or halt to walk, or trot to canter. Transitions can be **upward, (trot to canter), or downward, (canter to trot).**

Do transitions within gaits. Change the rhythm and the impulsion within the walk, trot, and canter.

THE BOTTOM LINE Doing *correct* upward and downward transitions as part of your daily flatwork is the key to making your horse's mouth soft and his back round and supple.

Doing transitions requires your horse to concentrate, change his footfall to the pattern of the new gait, and organize his body and balance for the transition. For the transition to succeed, you as a rider need to think about your own timing, balance, and organization.

Transitions within Gaits

Transitions within gaits aren't practiced nearly as much as between-gait transitions, but they should be. Doing transitions within gaits requires a bit more sophistication, in that it requires you to work at the rhythm (normal trot), under the rhythm (collection) and over the rhythm (extension) and always maintain impulsion.

It's difficult to go to a very slow trot without walking. It's difficult to move from an extended canter to a very collected canter without breaking to a trot. And a more forward walk might be difficult to achieve without breaking to a trot. Work on asking your horse to go from a short trot to a big trot, from collected to extended.

How Do Transitions Help?

Overall, transitions require that both horse and rider pay attention, manage their energy, and balance themselves.

Transitions help the horse balance. The change in the horse's footfall when transitioning between gaits and the

How Are Your Transitions?

There are a number of different exercises you can do that involve transitions. Try this one.

1. Walk 5 steps, then trot 10.

2. Walk 5 more, then trot 20.

3. Walk 10, then trot 10.

4. Walk 10, then trot 20.

5. Halt.

Ask yourself if your first steps in every pace were as good as your later steps. Keep practicing until you are consistent.

change in his center of gravity when making any transition result in a more level, more even weight distribution among all four hooves. Transitions can only be done properly if the hind end of the horse is underneath his body.

Transitions at specific points in the ring serve as mini-goals, which help focus the rider and organize her aids. As we discussed in section 3.1, having a clear goal, such as "go from a walk to a trot in the next corner," helps a rider prepare for and execute the goal better.

Practicing transitions helps your position. It's difficult to do transitions with a poor position — the odds of losing your balance during the transitions go up with every part of your body that strays from the classical position. For example, if you're leaning forward and try to do an upward transition from the trot to the canter, you're likely to produce a running trot that falls into the canter because your horse's weight will be on the forehand, not back on the hind end, where it needs to be to strike off into a graceful canter.

But if you're sitting up, with a straight line from your ear to your shoulder to your hip to your heel, with a straight line from your elbow to the horse's mouth, your body can support your horse as he shifts his weight to the hind end for the transition.

try this

You know how the quality of your horse's steps improves after you've been working for a while? **Keep that high-quality step in mind each time you ask for a transition. When doing a transition, try to make your first step as good as your fiftieth.**

Many riders will ask a horse to trot from a walk, **for example, and the horse will scuffle into the trot, dragging his feet, and looking as though, if the rider didn't keep kicking, he'd walk again. To fix this, think about making your first step of the new pace or gait be as good as your fiftieth step in that pace or gait will be. That means the first step isn't hurried or dragging – it's crisp and forward.**

What if your horse won't step right off into a crisp, bright new gait? **Then what? Use your stick or your spur. From the halt to the walk, ask your horse to step off by using your leg. If he doesn't respond, use the stick to reinforce the correct response to the leg. Your horse needs to understand and respect your leg. If you work through this lesson and arrive at a clear understanding from the halt to the walk, you'll find your horse is more obedient throughout your transitions at the other paces. (See page 15 for more on recalibrating your horse's response to your leg with the stick.)**

Riders who understand the power of transitions and know how to do them well are at a distinct advantage for the Intercollegiate Horse Show Association (IHSA) shows. In those shows, college riders must ride horses unfamiliar to them that are drawn by lottery. No warm-up work is allowed and riders must walk into the arena after mounting. Therefore, the transition from the walk to the canter for the opening circle in the arena plays a key role in establishing that the horse understands the rider's leg. It's quite a challenge, but if you know how to do an effective halt-to-canter transition, you can really have your horse responding to your leg before approaching your first fence.

You're Ready When: Picking the Right Time and Place

Always be sure you know when *is the right time to move on to the next part of your work.*

ONE VERY IMPORTANT THING about working on the flat (and with any work!) is knowing when, in each and every ride, it's time to move to the next thing. Knowing when involves a whole base of knowledge, rather than just a target. **Knowing when involves real horsemanship.**

True horsemen "know when" about a lot of things. They know to trot after warming their horses' muscles up at the walk first. They know that their horses' minds are ready for a tougher challenge when they're relaxed. They know if their horses' training has a hole to fill after the building blocks are in place. And they know when they themselves are safe and experienced enough for more of a challenge.

How Do You Know When You're Ready?

When *is* the right time? Surely we're not talking about a "right time" for something routine, something we do every day, are we? Well, yes. Everything has a time and a place. And it's your job as a horseman or -woman to learn about those right times and then to remember to ask yourself if you've reached that time in your work: in your daily work, in training your horse toward a larger goal, and in your career as a rider.

By asking your horse for more at the appropriate moments, you **set the stage for success** rather than failure.

THE BOTTOM LINE It's critically important to be sure your horse is ready before you ask him to answer a more advanced question.

In any given ride, ask yourself
these questions:

Q. When can I start my ride?
A. You start work after you
check that your girth is tight
and that your stirrups are the
correct length. Check in with your
horse — is he moving normally,
does anything seem to be bother-
ing him? Does he have the right
feel and usual mood?

**Q. When is it time to move to
another gait?**
A. It might be when your horse
is feeling heavy and dull, when a
change in balance will help him
carry himself better. It might be
when he's not paying attention,
when a focusing requirement will
be helpful. It might be when he's
feeling lovely at one gait and you
decide to "test" if that loveliness
is truly balanced.

**Q. When might my horse need
a reminder of our friendship?**
A. While we always want to make
friends with our horses, there will
also be specific times when your
horse might need an extra reminder
of that friendship. It might be when
he's uncomfortable with the pressure
of the exercise or with a new noise
outside the ring. It might be when
he's given an extra amount of effort
and needs to know you're pleased
with that. It may be when you've
had a hard day and you need to let
your horse know that your tension
has nothing to do with him.

**Q. When should I push my horse
a little harder?**
A. The time for this is after you
and your horse are physically
and mentally warmed up — and
when you are both performing
well. For example, you're ready to
ask for *extreme* extension and

Know When

Know when your horse's muscles are ready for more.

Know when your horse's mind is ready for more.

Know when your horse's training is ready for more.

Know when you are ready for more.

collection when you have properly executed *relative* extension and collection.

Q. **When am I ready to jump, in general or in a given ride?**
A. When you've accomplished the things transitions can help you with — balance, accuracy, timing, obedience, impulsion, and position — you're ready to jump. In addition, when you have a strong partnership with your horse, you're ready to jump. When your horse is relaxed and you're riding the whole body of the whole horse, you're ready to jump. When you've mastered the importance of having your horse accept and listen to your leg, you're ready to jump. Not before. That's a big list and a lot to accomplish, but when these basics are in place, your jumping will be more successful and, more importantly, safer!

Keep Asking

These types of "know when" questions should continue throughout your career as a rider, for each horse you ride. You'll be continuously faced with questions such as these: When is it time . . .

- To take off my stirrups and focus on my position?
- To include cavallettis in my work?
- To bring in a trainer?
- To get a different trainer?
- To start lateral work?
- To introduce water jumps?
- For my horse to have some down time?
- To back up in my training and reinforce simple concepts?
- To go to a show?

There's an answer to each of these questions, if you know the signs.

"Hindsight" by
Janet Crawford

4 | The Art of the Ride

Top level performances transcend sport; they are an art form.

AS RIDERS, WE'RE COMPLEX BEINGS. We're athletes. We're animal lovers. We're horse people. We're competitors. Some of us are trainers. Some of us are owners. **But artists?** That's not a word that's commonly used to describe riders.

Yes, artists. Every time we mount our horses, we're mounting not only as equestrian athletes but as artists. Art and music come together from little dots of paint and many different notes, from mechanical ability and trained skill, from emotion and touch — all coming together to create a beautiful painting or a wonderful song.

In this chapter we talk about the art of the ride and all the colors and dimensions that go into that masterpiece. We talk about the mechanics and the feeling involved with a good ride. We talk about the blending of the two that creates the harmony, the softness, the balance that results from a good ride — from an artful ride. We also talk about the art of making your horse feel as though each of your ideas was his own idea.

THE CONCEPT IN ACTION: Be an Artist Every Time You Ride | One of jumping's greatest artists was **Michael Matz,** who retired in 2000. Watching Michael, shown here on Olisco, ride was watching style at its very best. He knew how to get the most from a horse, while delivering an elegant ride in the classic American style. He painted a beautiful picture in each and every one of his rides.

As Michael showed us, good riding is an art. But in any form of art you need specific, mechanical skills along with the artist's creativity that allows the art to be created. We need those skills in riding as well. Let's zero in on just what we can do to perfect our artistic endeavor of riding, what we can do to perfect the Art of the Ride. It starts with becoming a mechanic — a good one.

First Become a Good Mechanic

Have the position and tools you need to give your horse the opportunity to perform well — and know how to use them.

WE'VE TALKED ABOUT a rider's aids and position, and we've covered a variety of fundamentals about riding your horse. Now let's look at how to execute those fundamentals of aids and position and how to actually use the pieces.

Start by imagining a cupboard in your kitchen or garage. To create things you mix ingredients. To be a good cook you need the right ingredients. To fix things you bring out your toolbox. **To be a good mechanic you need the right tools.**

Well, we'd like you to have a cupboard of riding ingredients or tools. For good riding you need some things you might be surprised to see in that cupboard. First, pull out the Jell-O and the fly tape. What will these tools or ingredients help you create?

The strangest ingredients make for the best ride: Jell-O, fly tape, and modeling clay!

What's Jell-O Got to Do with Anything?

We know how important position is and that good function follows good form. But what should your body do and how should you feel when placed into the correct position?

Jell-O used to have a commercial with a jingle that went something like, "Watch it wiggle, see it jiggle." You don't want to be wiggling all around

Reinforce with your leg what you want the horse's hind end to be doing. **Follow the rhythm with your seat.**

THE BOTTOM LINE Good mechanics are essential to create the art of the ride. Incorporate the mechanics of good riding every time you sit on your horse.

Flowing,
jiggly, soft,
relaxed –
moving like
Jell-O lets
you blend with
the motion
of the horse.

Stick to
that saddle
like a fly on
fly tape.

on top of your horse, and you don't want to be so rigid that you're bouncing on his back. You do want to **be relaxed enough to jiggle a bit within your correct position** to adapt to your horse's motion and movements.

This *doesn't* mean that you are moving all around up there. It means that your muscles aren't tense and flexed the entire time. Rather, they're relaxed and melting into your horse's back, in harmony with him. That way you can flow with the horse, rather than inhibit him through your stiffness.

What about the Fly Tape?

It sounds odd, but you need fly tape to go with the Jell-O. While you want to be able to soften your muscles and your body to be able to flow with

your horse, you also have to **think about sticking to your horse's back** no matter what. But you have to do it *softly*, in a three-point seat, with both seat bones sitting in the saddle. Ironically, the harder you try to stick, the more likely you are to stiffen and *not* be like Jell-O. But if you can get the Jell-O feeling first, the fly-tape feeling should come as you sink into your horse's back and follow his rhythm and energy.

Once your body is blended with the motion of your horse's gait, you can sit taller and heavier in the saddle to direct his movement. When you are tall and connected in the saddle, your seat can be more subtle in its ability to influence the horse's body. Having the mechanics

Stay on Track

While executing your changes of direction and changes in bend, it's important to keep your horse's body on the track. That means all parts of your horse's body exactly on the track, or path, that you're riding. For example, if you're riding a circle, every part of your horse's spine, from his poll to his withers to his croup to his tail, should be right on the line of that circle.

That's a tough task, because it's about being straight while bending. While following a curved line, your horse's body parts need to be straight behind one another following the same shape.

Jell-O and Fly Tape

This drawing shows the rider blending into the horse's motion by rounding and softening his back. Once his seat is in sync with the horse, he becomes taller by stretching up to influence his mount's movement. All along, his legs stick closely to the horse's sides as if he had fly tape on the inside of his legs.

Are You Riding Straight?

Think of riding straight as being similar to an insect or a butterfly collection. You know how the specimens are pinned to a Styrofoam block with their wings spread out? Ride your horse so that if he were pinned to Styrofoam at any point in your ride, all parts of his body would be exactly on the track that you're riding.

Try this: When riding a circle (or any other figure), think about hitting the pause button, so to speak, and freezing yourself and your horse at any moment on that circle. Now imagine an aerial photographer taking a picture of you and your horse frozen on your circle. If we were to put straight pins, from above, right through your horse's poll (between his ears), one through his neck, one through your saddle, one through his croup, and one through his tail, **would all the pins be on the arc of the circle**?

If you were riding a figure eight and we did the same thing just as you were changing direction, would your horse be soft and supple enough to be on the lines of the figure eight? On a serpentine? Right on the shape, in any direction, at all times? Comfortably?

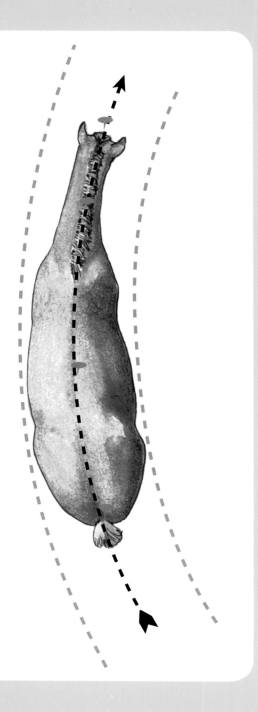

to blend your seat with your horse's motion allows you to use your seat for the art of the ride. A good seat becomes like an artist's high-quality paintbrush.

Bring Out the Modeling Clay

From Jell-O and fly tape to modeling clay? Think of it like this: When you first open a package of modeling clay and start working with it, it feels cold and stiff. But after you move it around and warm it up in your hands for a while, it becomes soft, flexible, supple . . . just as a horse becomes through good flatwork.

Having your horse be soft and supple is your goal. As you move through your flatwork, **you want your horse to feel more and more like modeling clay:** soft but firm, and able to bend his whole body smoothly from one side to the other. All parts of his body should be equally flexible so he can bend both ways evenly and change the bend effortlessly.

How do you make a horse into modeling clay? You accomplish it by moving, bending, and stretching the whole horse to get him soft and supple. You use your primary aids (legs and seat) to move, bend, and stretch his

Be a meticulous mechanic with the tools and ingredients in your cupboard: Jell-O, flypaper, modeling clay, and an insect collection!

try this

Have you ever ridden in the back of a truck or on the wheel well while going over a bumpy road? **If you stiffen your body, you'll be bounced right off the truck. But if you soften and relax your body, you absorb the bumps in the road. It's the same with your seat on the back of a horse.**

To make yourself one with your horse, you have to learn how to put your body into this state of relaxation and softness purposefully. **Otherwise, you'll be working against yourself the whole time. Stiffness makes riding an uphill battle.**

So try sitting the trot like you're on a wheel well of a truck driving over a bumpy road. **Relax like Jell-O and absorb the bumps to stick to the wheel well.**

body. You ask for a series of flatwork exercises at all the gaits, prioritizing changes of rhythm within each gait, stretching, leg yields, shoulder-ins, two tracks, shoulder-outs, bending, and upward and downward transitions. These all help produce a soft and supple horse.

Which tools? Which aids? What are the key things a rider can use to produce a soft and supple horse? You guessed it — the legs and educated use of the seat!

Remember that the primary aids are not effective without the coordinated use of the secondary aids — hands (reins), voice, and stick. We use legs, seat, and reins to ride a horse straight and forward, as well as to turn left and right. The legs (and seat) initiate and maintain each and every request we make with our horses. Our focus is to ride, manage, and direct the hind end of the horse, the engine!

How do you do that? Just as a mechanic can carefully diagram the flow of energy through an engine, you as an equestrian athlete can carefully map out your ride to incorporate changes of direction and bend. For example, you may plan your ride to go something like this:

- Track left twice around the ring
- Change rein across the diagonal
- Track right once around
- Circle right
- Change rein across the diagonal again
- Circle left
- Ride a serpentine of three loops
- Ride a half turn and reverse
- Ride another half turn and reverse

By riding with leg and a soft and sympathetic seat, and practicing many changes of direction and bend, and many upward and downward transitions, you can create a soft and supple horse. Like warmed-up modeling clay — supple but firm. Just right!

THE CONCEPT IN ACTION: Using Your Tools Well | Using the proper tools makes all the difference. Top international rider **Jessica Springsteen,** here riding Iscariote, knows how building that toolbox and learning to use the tools in it lead to the winner's circle. As a junior, Jessica won the ASPCA Maclay Medal Finals in 2008 using her tools effectively and precisely. In the final workoff the riders had to canter a single fence on the short side of the arena, then countercanter the next fence. While the riders before Jessica all jumped the jump, walked, then countercantered, she had the tools to make her horse land on the countercanter lead and continue on to the next fence.

A Little More Salt?
Or a Little More Sugar?

Riding is about opposites. A big part of being a rider is knowing how to answer the question, "What do you need, a little more salt or a little more sugar?"

Know what you
need to use:
A little
more salt?
Or a little
less sugar?

SALT. SUGAR. They're very different. Usually, people are more inclined toward one than the other. They taste different. They have different uses. Sometimes one agrees with us more than the other. And sometimes, we have only one available.

What do salt and sugar have to do with riding a horse? In riding you have to use all the tools and ingredients you have available to improve and fix things. And while some combination of tools might be ideal, there will always be some tools that you prefer or will be more effective using. Some tools suit you or your horse better.

So while you're more inclined to use certain tools, the one you choose may be just the opposite of the tool that's needed for the situation, because there will always be opposing forces at work with your horse. Specific examples of opposites crop up in riding all the time — you might say you want your horse to be "strong but soft" or "fast but composed" or "animated but relaxed."

For example, your horse may seem overly sensitive to the leg, so you think he needs less of it. In actuality he needs more of it. You may try to hold him back mostly with your hand, when really you should be adding leg to make him feel secure and balanced and give him a calming rhythm into which he can settle.

THE BOTTOM LINE Recognize the opposing and related tendencies within your horse and know the performance question at hand so you can answer the question correctly.

Are You Choosing the Right Solution?

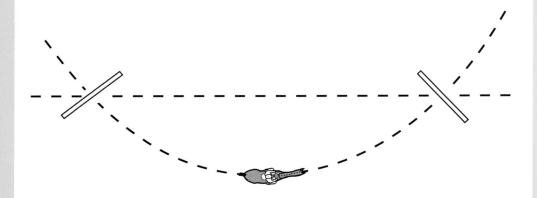

Think about where your strengths as a rider lie. Make a list. For example, are you better at soothing hot horses or at motivating lazy horses? Make a list for your horse as well. Is his stride length a gift or a liability? What about his straightness?

Once you have your lists, you can think about which direction you might more readily go when faced with decisions – will it be salt or sugar?

Here's a way to help you figure it out. Place two ground rails 60 feet (18 m) apart on a curve. Now plan how to canter these two poles first in five strides, then in seven. You have **two options** – adjust either your stride or your track. We'll cover this more in chapter 7, but for now, using the salt versus sugar idea, think about which mechanism you'd choose to get this exercise done.

Consider the lists you made that reflect your and your horse's strengths. Which is the better solution, stride or track? Make a clear choice, then go out and ride that choice.

If you choose stride, you'll primarily adjust your horse's stride from longer to shorter to get it done.

If you choose track, you'll ride a straight line between the fences for the five (stepping over them on an angle) and then add a larger bow, or push out more, between your fences to give yourself more room to make the seven work out.

While that is an example of a problem seeming to be one thing and the solution being something opposite, you may also encounter problems with solutions that aren't necessarily opposites but are different. Consider trying to jump a line with two fences that do not have a natural relationship because they are not in a straight line. Think about these tools:

- **TRACK.** Is your horse's body following the geometry of the exercise?

- **STRIDE.** Is your horse's stride the length it should be for the task at hand?

- **TRACK AND STRIDE.** Which one is your strength? Your horse's strength? How can you ride the line to best use that strength for a successful ride?

If your horse has a very adjustable stride but you aren't so strong about sticking to your track, then use the stride to help make the ride a success. If your horse's stride is not so consistent or adjustable, then really focus on nailing the track and making the ride a success by staying exactly on the path you choose.

Using Salt and Sugar

Salt or sugar is really about managing things that might oppose one another. Sometimes it's about choosing one or the other, and other times it's about how opposites work at the same time. Sometimes the use of one may drive the need to use the other.

Take for example a horse that canters faster and faster. Your first reaction is to sit more firmly and pull harder to slow him down, but it doesn't work! That's because your seat (the most influential aid you have) is telling the horse to go faster while your hands (secondary aids) are telling him to slow down. Guess what? Your seat instructions are much more dominant to the horse than your hands.

THE SOLUTION is often to neutralize your seat by removing it from the horse's back in a two-point. Without your seat driving him, the horse can "hear" your hands and slow down.

THE CONCEPT IN ACTION: Salt versus Sugar | **Katie Prudent** is an expert at blending, mixing, and matching the components of how a horse acts and goes to produce a perfect performance. Her use of touch, strength, and calm, combined with a fire within to win makes Katie a great "cook"! She knows how much salt and how much sugar is needed to bring out the best in a horse and turn in a winning performance. This innate gift was honed by her early years of tutelage under our sport's greatest teacher, George Morris, and it makes her one of the best coaches in the United States today. Here she is pictured in top form aboard Sassacaia III.

What a Feeling!

Feel what you're doing; don't look at what you're doing.

> Mechanically correct riding without feeling doesn't win ribbons, but riding only by feeling doesn't win either. You need both.

LOOKING DOWN WHILE YOU RIDE compromises your position, balance, and track. Keep your head up and your eyes looking forward; feel your ride instead of watching yourself ride. "Feeling" is one of those words that is used again and again in the horse world. It's talked about as if it's something people either have or they don't. If you're not born with it, too bad. It's the other end of the spectrum of being mechanical with your horse.

Some people do ride solely off feeling — they probably were born with some type of gift in this domain. Others riders ride solely from their minds and skills, their mechanics. But committing to the art of riding requires a blend of both. And we believe it's possible to develop feeling, just as you learn the mechanics.

Feeling with Your Seat

The discussion of riding like Jell-O in the previous section relates to feeling. It's a mechanical way to help make your body feel your horse, rather than stiffen up and lose the connection. Let's continue that discussion of letting your body feel your horse through relaxing your back and seat. It's tied in with the concept of use and nonuse of the seat in chapter 1. The use and nonuse of the seat is about knowing when to have your seat be a primary driving aid and when to put your seat into neutral.

Sometimes you might get that mixed up. Sometimes, you might *think* you're not using your seat but you're actually sitting back in the saddle, which means you *are* using it. Not only are you using your seat unintentionally, you could actually be driving your horse forward — or even driving him nuts!

THE BOTTOM LINE To become an artist in your riding, you need to develop feeling, not just learn the mechanics.

Consider this: Your horse or pony feels anxious and is misbehaving going back to the barn from the day's ride in the arena. As he's shaking his head in anticipation, and jigging, you sit down and up to make your seat more solid. But, as in the previous example of the cantering horse, your seat is a driving aid, so you're actually contributing to his energy level, inadvertently driving him forward too much.

This again may be a time to *not* use your seat — try a half seat and see if it helps your horse settle. The nonuse of the seat combined with a specific request, perhaps for a shoulder-in, that requires him to pay attention to you may solve your problem without causing a big fight.

Ride Your Horse's Mouth with Feeling

Have you ever heard an instructor say, "Take a *feel* of your horse's mouth"? What does feeling look like in that case? What does it feel like?

Taking a feel of your horse's mouth is about contact, but it's also about empathy. Feeling is empathy: constantly remind yourself that there is a living partner on the other end of the reins.

Feeling your horse's mouth means giving gently. It means being soft, not rigid. It means not flopping and pulling but resisting lightly, only increasing that resistance as needed. It means squeezing and releasing invisibly, understanding that the horse will feel the gentlest sensation.

Feeling is being in harmony with your horse. It's relaxed arms, like wet rope. It's well-oiled elbows and shoulders that follow the horse's head and neck as he walks and canters. It's fingers that stay closed but move to squeeze and relax on the

Know when to use the seat. Feel when to use the seat. Sometimes the *nonuse* of the seat is the better solution. That's salt and sugar in action!

> **Remember to breathe** and invite your horse to breathe as well!
>
> **Think of your horse's mouth, head, and neck as an extension of your own arms.**

reins to ask and reward the horse. Proper feeling becomes automatic, and your horse welcomes it.

Find Feeling in Your Arms

To have arms with feeling, **you must have elasticity in your arms.** They must be movable, not stiff and rigid. But they must move quietly and softly, like a rope or rubber band with gentle tension on it. It's a difficult concept for riders to work on and understand — but once you feel it, you'll never forget.

Without elasticity you aren't able to feel your horse's mouth as an extension of your own arms. Elasticity in the arms is impossible with locked elbows or stiff wrists. Try to have a gentle bend in your elbow, and think of your horse's mouth as part of your arms. Let your arms gently connect your lower back to his mouth, topline, and hind end while you remain soft, sympathetic, and relaxed.

Breathing Helps with Feeling

Much of feeling your horse involves breathing. Feeling requires relaxing through your middle (remember riding like Jell-O?), which is absolutely impossible while holding your breath.

Feeling involves being aware of your breathing and using it to help achieve your goal. When you hold your breath, you stiffen and close yourself off from feeling and connecting with your horse. The horse can feel that closing off, too. Feeling requires that nothing block your blending with the horse — so be sure to breathe out a lot while riding so you don't inadvertently block your ability to feel and blend with your horse.

Feeling is a tough concept to write about and hard to learn. While there are riders who seem like they're part horse themselves, it's possible for all of us to increase our feeling. **Keep trying. It will come.**

Breathing

Horses hold their breath too, so train yourself to notice your horse's breathing patterns. Explore ways you can get your horse to exhale when he's tense. One way is to take a few big, deep breaths yourself so that your horse can feel and hear you. He is likely to follow your example and exhale as well.

THE CONCEPT IN ACTION: Feeling Your Ride | **Todd Minikus**, a Grand Prix show jumper and alternate for the 2000 U.S. Olympic Show Jumping Team, is a natural rider. His feeling and intuitiveness come from being an animal lover and are reinforced by his past experience riding bulls. Todd, one of the few leading Grand Prix riders who did not come up through the equitation ranks, swears riding bulls is no different from riding horses (other than the control factor) and that a bull's buck mirrors a horse's jump.

His strength as a rider comes from understanding the emotions his mount is feeling at any given moment and knowing which emotions the horse needs to feel to compete and win. He excels at training his horses to be extremely rideable – to lengthen and shorten their strides, to turn tightly and accurately, and to accelerate and come back to him. His relationships with his horses are among the most precise and detailed in the world. Despite his atypical rider style, horses jump better for Todd than for most other riders in the world. Above, Todd is riding Pavarotti.

FOUNDATIONS OVER

Fences

Aaron Vale
on Quito in
Wellington,
Florida, 2011

5 | Make a Commitment

Right or wrong,

tell your horse

to do something.

The worst thing

to do is to give no

direction or make

no decision.

EQUESTRIAN ATHLETES KNOW about commitment. It helps us climb back on each time we fall. It gets us out of bed for those early morning warm-ups, feedings, and show preparations. It keeps us riding.

Horses know about commitment too. They like clarity and direction. They will try their hearts out for riders who give clear and definite cues when asking them to do something. Problems occur when instructions are given halfway, are confusing or contradictory, or aren't given at all!

But how does commitment help us ride more effectively? How does it help us grow as riders, as horse people, as leaders of this sport?

Commitment underlies all our efforts toward growth and improvement. In this chapter we discuss four fundamental areas that require a clear commitment for that winning ride to develop:

- Manage the emotions of the horse at all times
- Get closer to the jumps
- Ride the ride you know is right
- Use the "reset" button while jumping

As we move more clearly into jumping with this chapter and the rest of the book, we'd like to strongly emphasize that there is always, always, always the application of flatwork to jumping. Remember, jumping is flatwork with airborne moments!

Commit. Be Decisive.

Every time you ride your horse, whether you're jumping or working on the flat, commit to these things:

- Improve each and every time you ride. Don't accept the status quo; ask your horse to be better every time you ride.

- Learn what makes your horse go well and do his best. Use what works.

- Ride classically, even if your horse isn't going in a classical way or is not a classic athlete.

- Ride the body. Commit to having the body of the horse perform correctly, and you'll have a horse with a good mouth.

- Examine your performance relationship in terms of what might be missing.

- Utilize the emotional aids to manage the emotions of your horse.

- Wait at the jumps. Closer is better. Almost Always.*

- Execute the right ride: the right plan, the right pace, the best track.

- Use your "reset" button throughout your ride.

*NOTE: In the Hunter or Equitation Show ring, we aren't suggesting "Deep" spots — we'll cover appropriate pace and distance more in chapters 9 and 10.

THE CONCEPT IN ACTION: Emotional Commitment | In every ride, two-time Olympic Gold Medalist (2004 and 2008) **Beezie Madden** exemplifies commitment. Watch her carefully walk a course, then carefully execute her plan. Her commitment to classical riding shines through her textbook-perfect position no matter which horse she's on or the circumstances she faces. Here she demonstrates her commitment to perfect form, feeling, and focus on her mount Via Vola.

Emotional Commitment Comes First

Use your emotional toolbox to manage the emotions of your horse so he can relax and engage in his work.

A relaxed horse is a rideable horse. He performs and jumps better and more consistently.

AS SEASONED RIDERS we've all been exposed to the different mechanical aspects of riding: using our aids and learning the mechanisms for getting our horses to go, stop, and turn. We have "tools" for all these actions. Through our years of riding, we've created a mechanical toolbox. In that toolbox we have our heel down, our leg, our seat, our hands, and our eyes.

There's another toolbox: the emotional toolbox. The emotional toolbox holds the tools used to manage the emotions of our horses to help them relax and engage in their work. Emotional tools include things like remembering to keep breathing, using a calming voice, relaxing your own body, neutralizing the seat, and tuning into to the horse's body language.

Think about this: Horses typically will gain speed and energy as they proceed through their course. Very few horses will jump the last four fences of a course as quietly as they did the first four fences of the course. Why? Because jumping is an emotional experience for the horse — more so for some horses than for others.

Horses can get worked up. Nervous. Worried. Your horse's natural instinct is to run away from anything that frightens or upsets him. When you're riding, you need to manage

THE BOTTOM LINE In addition to the mechanical aids, you need to have emotional aids in your toolbox to manage your horse's emotional experience during training, riding, and competing.

those natural instincts. Your job as emotion manager is to settle the emotions that arise so your horse can perform to the best of his ability.

Accomplishing this means that you must commit to recognizing situations that might cause your horse to worry, as well as recognizing your horse's emotional state. Your horse depends on you to protect him and guide him. As an animal of flight, he needs to know that you'll keep him safe from things that "go bump in the woods." He needs to have confidence in you, so you need to have confidence in yourself. And we need to ride with special aids for managing our horse's emotions — emotional aids.

Let Your Horse Speak to You

Be sensitive to your horse's emotions and reactions. Listen to his energy and feel his emotions each and every time you ride. Go back to the list of questions in chapter 2 (pages 33 and 34) and see if those signs of emotion are present in a jumping situation. They may, indeed, be compounded. Because it introduces a new layer of complexity to the ride, jumping can excite or scare a horse more than regular flatwork. Similarly, if the horse is in pain or lacks confidence at the jumps, jumping will elicit different emotions that need to be recognized and managed by the rider.

Consider your horse's emotions while jumping by asking yourself additional questions, such as these:

- Does my horse tense up when trotting into a ring filled with jumps?

- When trotting a spooky jump, does he snort and shy away?

- When cantering a pole on the ground, does his demeanor change (faster breathing, quicker steps, tenser muscles)?

- When trotting over a crossrail, does he pin his ears?

- Does he want to buck after each jump? Is he running away from the jump or just playing?

Asking these questions when jumping allows you to recognize your horse's emotions, then helps you know how to manage them. Answering "yes" to the questions above points to a nervous or tense horse that needs to be calmed and settled.

How do you do that? Quite simply, if you relax, your horse relaxes. And how do you relax? It helps to give your horse something to focus on other than what he is stressing

Commit to managing your horse's emotional experience. Commit to using emotional aids.

over. Here are some tried and true methods:

Take big, deep breaths. You've heard it before, but it works. When you're tense, your horse is tense. Deep breathing releases tension and helps you and your horse focus.

Take his mind off the monster. When your horse is scared or stressed about something (a particular jump or a spooky part of the arena), occupy his attention by giving him something else to do and concentrate on: a bend, a transition, a leg yield, or a change of direction. Keep his brain and body busy so as to minimize his focus on what is disturbing him.

Be aware of your feelings. Managing your own emotions isn't always easy. You have to be honest about your mind-set each time you get on your horse and learn to cope with outside pressures, stressors, and fear. It's not simple, but it's well worth it.

Consider your anchor point.
A key part of using an emotional toolbox is thinking about where we anchor ourselves from each time

we apply an aid. Ask yourself this question: "How much pressure do I use when I first apply an aid?" From a "managing the emotions" perspective, the answer to that question should be zero. You start with zero degrees of pressure and gradually increase the amount of leg, seat, and hand pressure as needed to get the reaction or results you are asking for.

Give your horse a chance to be good. When you start your work, assume your horse will be good. Instead of looking for what's wrong, look for what's right about the way he's working. Always *ask* your horse for what you want; don't force him. Create the opportunity for your horse to succeed. Find opportunities to reward and celebrate his performance throughout each ride.

Horses Can Be Too Quiet

Usually, we think of using our emotional aids to soothe and relax a fresh, tense, or scared horse. But that assumes that the only emotions horses experience are ones that require soothing and calming them down.

When applying aids, **start with zero degrees of pressure** and gradually increase as needed.

Commit to
sharpening
the tools in
your emotional
toolbox.
Know how
to relax
your horse
or wake him up,
as needed.

Sometimes managing your horse's emotions means focusing on something other than "work." Going out for a good gallop or a relaxing trail ride can refresh both you and your horse and renew your commitment to jumping.

Focusing on
the positives
relaxes and
soothes both
horse and rider,
inviting more
positive experi-
ences to come
your way.

We all know there's more to horses than that — yes, they are prey animals, and they can get scared and nervous, but many horses need us to help them on the "go" side instead of the "whoa." They might be lacking motivation. They might be lazy, tired, or just bored with their job. They may naturally be slow.

Whatever the reason, **there are many times we need to use the go button**. How? Other than the stick and spur, how can we help the go button?

Know your own go button. Are you naturally "hot" or "cool"? Do you prefer a calm, controlled canter in an arena or a free-flowing gallop outside with the wind in your face? Is it hard or easy for you to unleash and move into a fast gallop? Knowing the answers to these questions is important, and it's important to be honest with yourself about how readily and confidently you can inspire your horse and allow him to be what he is naturally — a playful, galloping animal.

Make sure your horse enjoys his job and feels good about doing it. There's no better way to do that than to spend riding time allowing him to open up his step and enjoy being ridden.

Have fun with your horse. Make his training experience interesting. Vary the job, the terrain, and the intensity of the "good job" after the fence or the exercise. Show your horse that it's fun to run for the timers, that it's fun to try extra hard over a bigger jump. **Laugh.** Share your own excitement about the task, and your horse will sense it and feel it, too.

try this

Pretend you're done. **You know how when you're done with your course and you let your body soften, you breathe out, and you soften your hands? Your horse walks, takes a big breath, and relaxes. Give your horse that ride every time you land from a fence. Whenever you jump a fence, ride like you're done. Breathe. Invite your horse to relax.**

THE CONCEPT IN ACTION: Emotional Commitment | **Chase Boggio** is pictured here in excellent position on his Young Rider mount, Hennessey. What Chase does best is sense and manage his mounts' emotions. In all three rings – hunter, equitation, and jumper – he encourages his horses to "take a breath" and relax, enabling them to perform beautifully. Chase leads by example, passing to his mounts the emotions he needs from them so they perform at their best. By staying relaxed, calm, and composed, and always being gently connected with his legs and seat, he encourages the horse to relax and focus. It is uncanny how the "emotional aids" influence a horse's performance, and Chase's gift has contributed to his sterling junior career. His presence and effect on a horse is an excellent example of a rider who manages the emotions of a horse.

Closer Is Better, Almost Always

Work on honing your eye to help your horse find the sweet spot.

It's okay to get close to the jump. It's easier and safer!

DEEP SPOT. LONG SPOT. Perfect spot. When you ride to a fence, you have a range of possible places for the takeoff to occur. Sometimes you know where that place will be, sometimes you don't — you have to take the spots as they come. With practice you can make those perfect spots come your way on a more regular basis.

Despite practice you will encounter fences at less than optimal distances. So you must make a commitment to being patient with your eye and not forcing the takeoff spot. Why? Because closer is almost always better. **Why is closer better?** It's **easier** for your horse to jump from a distance that is too close than from one that is too far. That makes it **safer**. Period.

"Wait, wait, wait." You've heard it before. In every warm-up ring at every horse show, you'll hear these words. Trainers call them again and again to their clients. Riders say them over and over again in their heads. But waiting is hard to commit to. What's the secret? To resist the temptation of those big, bold, long spots that may be screaming your name, you need to commit to two things: being patient and staying in balance.

The secret lies in being patient. Commit yourself to focusing on being patient on every ride. Commit yourself to making your mind overrule your body. Commit yourself to staying in the rhythm and allowing the distance to present itself.

THE BOTTOM LINE A closer distance to the jump is almost always better, so develop strategies that increase your ability to pass up the long ones and allow the more practical takeoff spots to present themselves.

The next thing is staying in balance.
You can do that by keeping your body with the motion and centered in the middle of the horse. Stretching up into this jumping position helps you stay in balance with your horse and helps your horse maintain the balance he needs to jump effectively and safely.

For a horse to get close to a fence, his weight must be back on the hindquarters — he has to compress his body, sit down more on his hocks, and propel up and over the jump. For your horse to do that, you have to help. If your weight is too forward in anticipation of the jump coming, then your horse can't shift his weight to the back where it needs to be.

No More "Long Eye"
A **long eye** means having a love for the wild spots. For the feeling of kicking and surging off the ground from almost a stride away. Those wild spots can be fun — they get your blood pumping, that's for sure. But you need to avoid them. Jumping wildly can get you and your horse hurt and makes you more likely to incur penalties.

Being patient and stretching up will help keep you from developing a long eye or will help you undo it if you've already got one. Commit to

undoing that long eye, that urge for the wild spot. Commit to getting closer. Be patient, stretch up, and think about cantering up to the jump and stepping over it.

It takes time to learn to be patient and stretch up. Jimmy Williams, former USET coach, AHSA Horseman of the Year, and Show Jumping Hall of Fame inductee, used to say, "It takes as long to undo something as it did to do it."

> **Don't force the jump** to happen. Be patient. Trust that a good jump will result.

> **The jump is just another canter stride.**

Stretch Up for Energy
Stretching up gives the horse support, impulsion, and the balance he needs to jump. It signals him to keep his hind end engaged. Think about it: When you want your horse to walk at the end of a course, do you stretch up? Nope. You collapse your body and breathe . . . you think about being Jell-O. But when you stretch up, you prepare your horse to pay attention and perform.

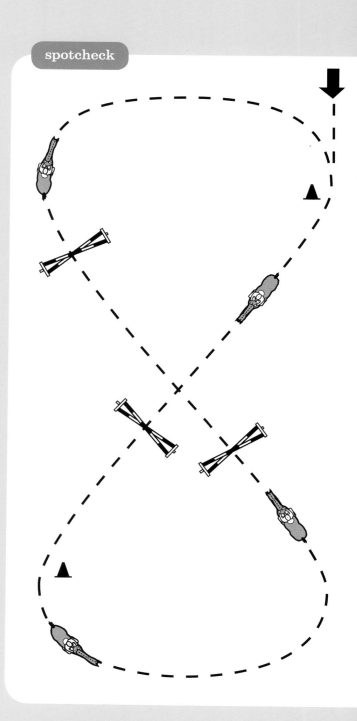

try this

Place a rail on the ground in the middle of the arena. Hold your lead as you canter over the rail. This will only happen if your horse is stepping over the rail and not jumping it. It's great practice for developing horse and rider patience.

Are You Waiting Patiently?

The best way to learn to wait patiently for the fence is to set a very simple course of three small cavaletti in a figure-eight pattern. Canter the three cavaletti on the figure eight, first with your horse's normal stride, then with a bigger stride, and then with a shorter stride. Having to wait for the fences regardless of your pace (stride and length) is a difficult thing to learn, and practicing this exercise will help develop that patience and rhythm.

But how will you know what a short, normal, and big stride feels like? Here's how:

- Start with your normal stride and count how many strides you take from one cavaletti to the next.

- Based on that stride length, rate your horse so that you can do one additional stride between the two cavaletti.

- Then encourage him to move out a bit more so that you take one less stride, relative to your normal stride, between the two cavaletti.

There are several goals in doing this exercise:

1. Be able to ride at that stride length on demand to do the "normal," "short," or "long" strided numbers between the two cavalletti.

2. Maintain the given stride length over the single cavaletti.

3. To do the exercise three times without stopping, doing a different stride length each time.

You will be able to do this waiting exercise successfully if you are patient with your eye and comfortable working out of different length strides.

Make Each Jump Work

Having an "eye" at the jumps has nothing to do with your actual eyes. It has to do with your stride and your track. It's that simple.

> **To see a distance,** you want and need stride, track, rhythm, and balance.
>
> **Don't neutralize your horse's ability** to get himself over a fence.

Distance: "That was a great distance to that oxer." "I blew that distance." "I just didn't see anything at all to that fence." "For the life of me, I can't see a spot to a jump." "How is it that you always see your spot?" "When I came out of that corner, I just saw where I needed to be at that fence."

We talk about distance all the time. And we talk about our "eye" for a spot, for a distance to a jump that is most ideal.

Newsflash: "Seeing your distance" is not about using your eyeballs. A good distance is about your leg and seat riding the body of the horse. It's about track and stride. It's about being patient. It's about cantering down to the jump and allowing a reasonable

takeoff spot to present itself. And it's about not getting in your horse's way.

Seeing your distance is about being able to ride a variety of different distances — meaning different *relative* distances — depending on the fence, or the question, at hand.

To find a good distance, you need to do the following:

- Have your horse truly riding from back to front
- Ride with connection
- Ride with rhythm
- Keep your horse straight
- Stay in the rhythm and allow the distance to materialize without pulling

THE BOTTOM LINE To arrive at the optimal takeoff distance to a jump, concentrate on your track and stride and allow the takeoff spot to present itself.

When jumping, always be looking ahead to the next obstacle. Discipline your eye to focus on where you're going, not where you are.

Sometimes, just thinking about the concept of "seeing a distance" a little differently helps riders. Here are some things to think about the next time you're riding to a jump:

- Try for a little distance by just cantering up and stepping over the jump.

- Look at the jump all the way through the turn.

- Allow the distance to present itself; allow the jump to present itself.

- You don't want to be at the end of your gallop (with your horse cantering on his forehand).

- You don't want to be in first gear or third gear; you want to be in the middle gear so you can either hold up or ride up. In first gear you are already holding up and cannot hold up any more. If you're at the end of your gallop and you need to push your horse a little, you can't because you're already there.

The top riders make the imperfect distances work out.

With any one of these elements missing, you're likely to have a less than lovely fence. You might chip, where your horse falls on his forehand and squeezes in a tiny little step just at the base of the fence. Or worse, you'll have a stop.

But when all those things are in place, you'll have the distance that you've been trying to *see*. And it's not seeing with your eyeballs. Seeing a distance results when a horse is rideable and balanced down to the jump.

When track, stride, balance, and connection are correct, the actual takeoff spot is less important. A little long or a little deep doesn't matter because all the important parts of the ride are in place.

spotcheck

Can You Discipline Your Eye?

Do you ever feel as though you see nothing sometimes, then at other times you see a long, wild spot? Well, here's an exercise that will force you to focus on your riding and not look at the jump:

- Set two ground poles on a 20-meter circle as shown.

- Canter the poles, staying on the circle.

- Imagine that the circle is a clock, and keep your eyes looking at the equivalent of 20 to 30 minutes ahead of where you are.

- Canter two or three circles, keeping your eyes ahead the whole time. Walk, then reverse the exercise.

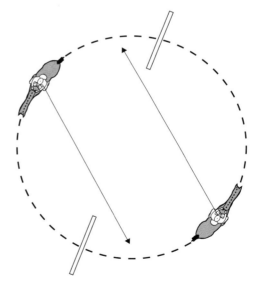

Requiring your attention to be ahead will keep you balanced and will require your leg to maintain your horse's impulsion and body on the track. Your peripheral vision will pick up the fence, but your mind will learn to wait patiently until the natural arrival at the jump occurs.

Ride the Ride You Know Is Right

You have enough sense and experience as an athlete to understand the exercise and stick to the plan.

YOU'VE WALKED THE course; you know the strides. You know the place you'd like to land from fence 1, and you've identified the gap through which you're going to ride afterward. So you know what the right ride is.

But how often have you entered the ring and left the right ride behind? You turn too early and approach a fence from the wrong angle. Or you were planning to jump on the perpendicular and ended up jumping on an angle. It's very easy for **our minds to convince us that we're doing a good job out on a course (even when we aren't!)**, that we have a nice approach, when in fact we've left the rail to approach the jump a good 14 feet before we were planning to!

So far, we've talked about how riding involves a complex kind of knowing, feeling, and seeing. But it also involves discipline and a commitment to riding the ride that you know is the right ride — the right track, the right geometry. **Riding the ride you know is right requires the discipline of an athlete.** Commit to building that discipline.

Riding the ride you know is right means managing your own impulse to randomly execute a different plan. Commit to identifying what you know is right on any given ride and whether you're really riding that ride. Commit to that truth, to what you *know* works. Commit to the track, to the stride, to executing the ride that you know is right.

Don't just hope things will work out: **Create a plan and stick to it!**

It's your job to be a leader and lead your horse to the right ride.

THE BOTTOM LINE Always strive to ride the ride you know is right — for your horse, for the question posed, and for you.

Are You On the Right Path?

Leaders clear the path for their people. Good riders clear the path for their horses: they plan the path to success and make sure their horse is on it. Here's an exercise to help you stay on the right path:

- Set up two intersecting lines across the ring, as shown. Use markers, such as a helmet or cone on the fencepost or a big X in duct tape on the wall, to identify the end points of both lines.

- Ride your horse through the exercise, going down each line and changing directions.

- As you turn onto each line, halt at the Xs shown and look at where you are relative to your targets.

- Ask yourself: Am I riding the line I know is right? Am I leading my horse through the exercise, following the track?

Now try this: Using the same lines, set up small jumps. When you jump, can you still reach your targets?

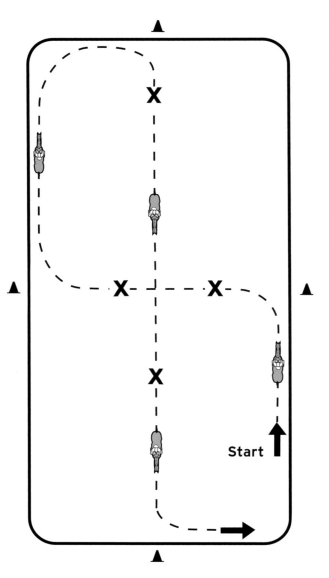

THE CONCEPT IN ACTION: Riding the Ride You Know Is Right | In the 2010 World Cup Qualifier at Wellington, Florida, one line represented everything that was needed to win for that course: A normal five-stride line from an open water to a tight vertical-to-vertical combination with a reverse Liverpool at the B element. **Mario Deslauriers** won by knowing and executing the ride he knew was right instead of doing what the other competitors were doing. Although the line walked a normal five, Mario knew he had to do six short strides in order to clear the very tight vertical-to-vertical in-and-out. Trusting his instincts and experience, he did the short strides masterfully and jumped clear, winning on Urico, shown above.

Reset

The half-halt: being able to reset your balance and connection while on course is critical to your success.

Learn how to do a half-halt and when to use it.

Reset. Esc. Ctrl/Alt/Delete. These buttons allow us to pause what we've created and have a momentary fresh start. Well, why should our riding be any different? Earlier we talked about keeping the building of pace from occurring throughout a course and how the emotional aids can help navigate that increase. A key part of managing your pace throughout a course is the **reset button**.

The reset button is the half-halt, however subtle or strong it needs to be. It involves using your legs and lower body to briefly sit against the mouth of the horse with your reins. The half-halt plays a critical role on course that helps you and your horse **regroup, readjust, rebalance, and reaffirm** your focus and your job. It helps you stay organized and maintain the desired stride, balance, and focus to answer the next jumping question.

So when do you actually use this button? Once you learn the values of the half-halt, you will find yourself using it often. Examples include when your horse gets strong, built up, or on the forehand. Other instances might be after riding a forward line or negotiating a spooky jump. The **key to the half halt is to use it as soon as the need arises**, not ten strides later. While there are specific, strategic locations relative to the fences and the course where the reset button should be used (which we'll cover below), we'd like to first answer the question of how you actually push the reset button.

THE BOTTOM LINE Balancing your horse with half-halts on the flat and over fences gives you an effective "reset" button to use when jumping a course.

In hunters and equitation divisions, the reset should be invisible to any person watching. If your hunter or equitation horse is well schooled you won't need a strong half-halt, just a subtle one done with less strength and fewer visible movements. When done well, it's a moment of "How are we doing?" between you and your horse, with the resultant answer of "We're great — we're balanced, checked in, and working together."

Half-Halt: Hitting the Reset Button

To reset, do the following, all at the same time:

- Stretch up tall in the saddle.
- Bend your horse slightly.
- Close your legs.
- Lift up your horse's head by bracing against the forward momentum of the gait.
- Straighten and relax.
- Repeat as needed.

try this

Ask your horse to canter a small fence on the long side. **After landing and about four strides before the corner, practice the half-halt. Then gently give and allow your horse to continue his canter stride and enter the corner. When this is done correctly, you'll feel your horse lighten significantly and really shift his weight back. Be careful, though — without the leg to continue asking for the canter, your horse will trot!**

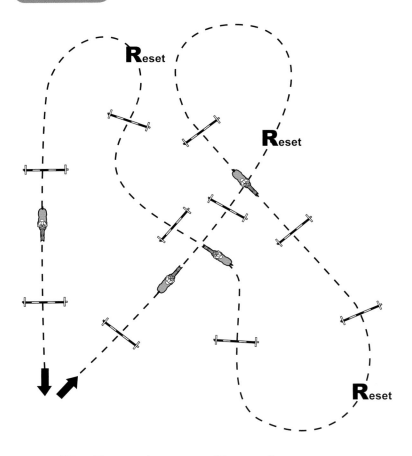

Are You Resetting over Fences?

Place 10 small fences in an area as shown above (or use as many as you can in the space you have). At the points indicated, reset your horse's balance by doing a half-halt. If you do this exercise correctly, your horse will maintain his pace and rhythm and stay relatively light throughout the course instead of building speed and getting more on his forehand.

If you pass a reset point without successfully resetting, just circle and try again. The circle gives you time to repeat the half halt until you can maintain your horse's balance and forward momentum.

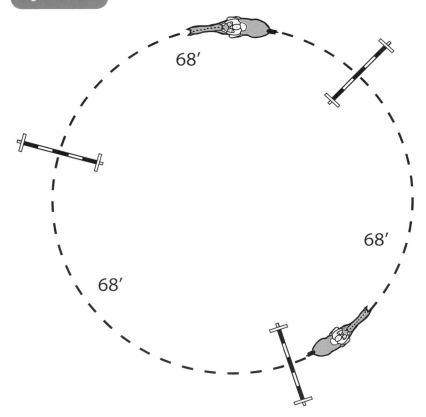

Are You Committed to Your Stride?

A wonderful way to spot-check commitment is the circle exercise. Though at first glance it appears simple, it can be quite challenging to do in the same number of strides between each fence. The circle exercise will challenge your commitment to managing the emotions of your horse; to getting close to your jumps; to riding the ride you know is the right ride; and to resetting, or half-halting, your horse.

To ride the circle exercise, set three small fences in the pattern above. There should be five quiet strides, or 68 feet, between the fences. However, depending on the track and geometry you ride, you may end up with more or fewer strides in between jumps. With practice and commitment, though, you can be sure that it will eventually work out well!

6 | Jumping Gymnastics

Gymnastics are absolutely fundamental to developing balance, technique, and strength in both horse and rider.

EQUINE GYMNASTICS RESEMBLE the human sport in their focus on power, agility, flexibility, and technique. We may not use a balance beam with horses, but we do use uneven bars, in the form of jumps. Gymnastics with horses involve jumping a series of fences of varying heights and widths in close, consecutive order.

Gymnastics look different depending on the goal of the exercise. For example, to help a horse increase his ability to jump obstacles from both a short and a long stride, the distances between several of the fences may be short and between others, long. That's the beauty of gymnastics: because the jumps

What Are Gymnastics?

In the horse world, the term "gymnastics" refers to a series of jumps set up in a straight or curved line with specific distances between them. The jumps are configured to focus on particular issues to improve horse and rider over jumps.

Use gymnastics to isolate and improve your jumping ability and technique.

are so carefully measured out, the exercise isolates issues and helps both horse and rider improve.

In this chapter we discuss how gymnastics help a rider's position and technique, then move to an overview of how they help both horse and rider with balance, timing, and adjustability. You'll find three specific gymnastic exercises at the end of the chapter, for both novice and advanced horses and riders.

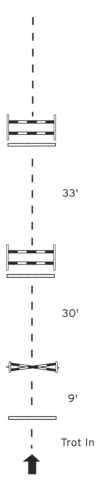

33'

30'

9'

Trot In

A very basic gymnastic course requires a minimum of six jump standards and seven poles; you can manage with just two jumps, but three (as shown here) is preferable. With this setup, practice trotting over the cross-rail and cantering to the verticals on a dead straight line. Concentrate on a focal point at the end to help stay centered.

Result: Perfect Position

Keep your body tall and let your horse jump up to you.

WE'VE TALKED A LOT about how a correct position helps you use your aids properly and be more effective as a rider. That holds true when working on the flat and when working over fences. Gymnastics provides **a golden opportunity to focus on your position** as a rider. It minimizes variables, giving horse and rider a consistent, reproducible question where the only variables are technique and performance.

Gymnastics gives you the chance to become familiar with the motion and movements your horse uses to jump and for you to complement his efforts by fine tuning how you use your upper body and how you manage your weight distribution over jumps.

In case of short distances, gymnastics helps you think about stretching up and letting your horse jump up to you, fence after fence, right in a row. Practicing that feeling in a gymnastics helps you reproduce that feeling when presented with that question in the show ring.

With the fences right in a row, gymnastics helps you improve on your position during takeoff and landing, as well as in the air. It gives you the opportunity to focus on your **heels** and **legs, eyes, back,** and **release**.

Your Heels and Legs

Remember this from chapter 1? "When you know what to do, put your weight in your heels. When you don't know what to do, put your weight in your heels." Well, gymnastics give you the perfect opportunity to focus on

Gymnastics is a **simple investment** of time and effort for a **huge return** in performance.

THE BOTTOM LINE Gymnastics can help both horse and rider sharpen their form and performance over fences.

pushing your heels down by eliminating the need to navigate turns, set the right pace, and figure out approaches.

The straight "chute" aspect of a gymnastic exercise also allows you to focus on using your leg to keep your horse straight down the middle of that chute. If you are not using your legs equally, your horse will drift, finishing to the left or right of where he started. **Use your legs to steer through the chute** from the center of one jump to the center of the next.

Remember to put equal weight in each heel, aiming for centered weight distribution and balance through the entire exercise.

Your Eyes

Gymnastics gives you the chance to keep your eyes targeted on a focal point, usually a spot above and beyond the straight line of the gymnastics. When you commit to a focal point, your body and position instinctively become more centered and balanced.

Your Back

Your back and upper body benefit from consecutive fences in two ways. In the case of a short distance, your upper body has to stretch up and allow the horse to jump up to you. In the case of a long distance, your upper

---

spotcheck

How's Your Position?

Set up the Novice gymnastics on page 123 and have someone videotape you from the very end of the line with you coming toward the camera, then from the side of the exercise. Evaluate your position, asking these questions:

- Are your heels down throughout the entire exercise?

- Are your eyes up and committed to your focal point?

- Are you keeping your horse straight with your legs?

- Are you closing your upper body to help your horse's efforts?

- Are your hands quiet and not catching your horse's mouth or rushing his jump?

body should follow the motion of the canter and reinforce the lengthening of stride as well as the push off the ground. For riders who "throw their bodies" and break over too much, work in gymnastics provides the opportunity to slow the body down.

Your Release

Gymnastics will also help your release. As you go over each jump, think about the type of release you typically use. Especially think about whether you catch your horse in the mouth while you're in the air or on takeoff or landing. Gymnastics will help you review your release and improve your ability to give your horse the freedom he needs and deserves while jumping.

The drawings on the next two pages illustrate some of the ways in which gymnastics can help a rider's position.

Reviewing the Release

When jumping, your hands and arms should follow the horse's neck and allow it to stretch out and down over the jump. This movement of following the horse's head and neck in the air while jumping is called the release.

While we don't cover the different types of releases in detail, we urge you to consider your release and the type of release you typically use. Developing riders should use a crest release, while more advanced riders move to an automatic release. And we recommend you read George Morris's work for more information about them.

Building Your Position with Gymnastics

A. Approaching the Jump

A. Both horse and rider are balanced and in correct position, with ears and eyes focused on the jump ahead.

B. Here the rider is using a crest release and is in good form, although I would like to see her back a little straighter.

C. This is a good example of position and balance on landing – note how correctly the rider's weight is absorbed in her deep heel.

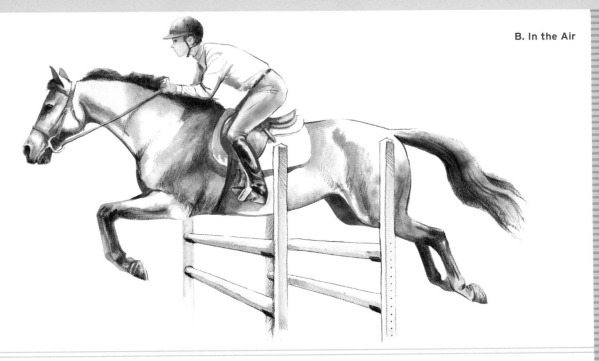

B. In the Air

C. Landing

Result: Balance and Timing

Gymnastics force the horse to organize himself and not rely on his rider to help him along.

Use gymnastics to help both you and your horse **develop better balance and technique.**

TWO VERY IMPORTANT elements for both horse and rider to have when jumping are **balance** and **timing** — two very difficult elements to practice and get right, but they can *definitely* be learned and improved upon. Gymnastics don't only help *your* position and form, they also help your horse's form over fences. As your horse concentrates on the distances between the fences, he learns to use his body more effectively. Working on gymnastics not only helps your horse with his balance and timing, but also his technique and the shape of his arc over the jump.

Gymnastics help a horse develop greater balance by requiring that he organize himself and not rely on his rider for constant guidance. In a gymnastics exercise **the horse is relatively on his own.** There aren't many options except to find his balance and jump well — all other options involve some level of discomfort (e.g., knocking down the fence). In the case of a single fence with a long approach, there are other options, such as rushing, leaving long, adding strides, running out, approaching the fence crooked, and so on. All those possibilities are virtually eliminated with gymnastics. Once in, a horse has to carry on and jump out.

By having to carry on and jump through the exercise, the horse quickly learns to react to the obstacles in front of him. The

THE BOTTOM LINE Gymnastics allow a horse to develop his own sense of balance and timing in jumping.

setup of the fences actually tells the horse how to find his balance, because the tighter distances that are typically found in gymnastics require that he collect himself and keep his weight distributed more toward the back end. Having his weight shifted off his front end enables the horse to gather his front end up and over the fence again and again, as required by the exercise. A gymnastics with relatively short distances teaches a horse to balance himself at and between the fences.

In learning to balance himself, **the horse also learns timing**. The timing for jumping — as with the timing between fences — is determined by the spacing of the elements in the exercise. These things are best learned in the isolated, focused environment of a gymnastic exercise.

spotcheck

Are You Managing Your Horse's Energy?

Set up the gymnastics on page 123 that is the most appropriate for you and your horse's level of development (novice or advanced). Think about your horse's balance from the moment you cross over the first pole on the ground.

Resist the temptation to help your horse. Let the exercise do its job and help your horse find his own balance.

Imagine your horse's point of balance underneath you. See if you can feel it shifting back farther each time you go through the gymnastics.

Stay in balance with your body. Allow your horse to jump up to you for the short distances and follow the push of his jump for the long distances.

Result: Adjustability

You want your horse to be like a spring: able to load from back to front and adjust in length.

Gymnastics teach a horse to use the correct bascule over different jumps.

IF YOUR HORSE CAN ACT like a big spring, he is able to adjust easily and fluidly in his approach, takeoff, and landing at each jump, from short to long and back, again and again. To be able to adjust like this, your horse needs to learn how to shorten and coil his jumping stride (his "spring") as well as lengthen and elongate it. And you need to develop his muscles to give him the power and the balance to be able to adjust his body.

Gymnastics helps your horse learn how to load his spring, how to shorten and lengthen his body at the jumps for things like a better, closer takeoff and covering more (or less) ground in between the jumps.

How Do Gymnastics Develop the Spring?

Gymnastics help a horse develop his spring by requiring that he adjust his stride and balance a number of different times within any given exercise. By setting **different distances between the jumps** within the gymnastics, you require the horse to lengthen and shorten his body accordingly.

You can also help your horse learn to use his body like a spring by choosing the type of fences that are set throughout the exercise. The demands of a simple vertical fence, for example, are different from those of an oxer made of large Xs.

THE BOTTOM LINE Gymnastics teach your horse to be more adjustable in both his length of stride between jumps and his arc over them.

Here the gymnastic puts the horse close to the jump, forcing him to "load his spring" and put his hind end underneath himself to power over the jump.

Here the gymnastic requires the horse to lengthen his stride between jumps and elongate the spring.

This horse's arc is nicely centered over the oxer, even though he is jumping "flat backed," meaning that the length from his shoulder to his hip is flat rather than slightly rounded.

Talking about Arc

When talking about the shape of the horse's body and flight path over a jump, we refer to it as the **arc or bascule**. Different fences require different arcs. You want your horse to be adjustable and able to jump any fence regardless of the arc it calls for.

Gymnastics help a horse and rider learn how to do this. As you practice over elements with a variety of shapes, your horse will learn to jump fences with different arcs. He'll learn to anticipate what bascule is needed at each jump with subtle cues that you've established during gymnastic exercises.

When watching a horse jump, think of an Etch A Sketch toy. Imagine that your horse is going over a jump and the Etch A Sketch captures what his arc looks like. With an educated horse, the arc will look like this, with the jump in the center.

While different types of fences may encourage a different arc, you want to produce the same round bascule whether you jump from a close spot or a long one, as shown here.

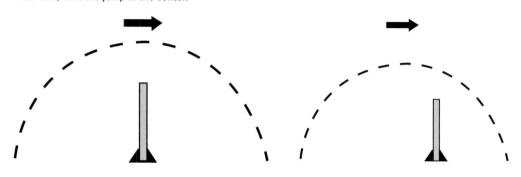

The same holds true for all different types of obstacles, like the triple shown here.

As with the vertical, you should strive to produce the same arc from even the closer spot.

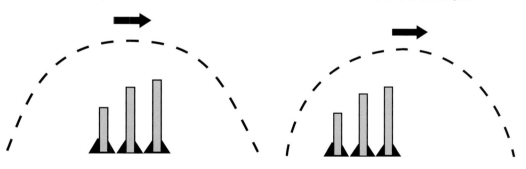

Sharing Subtle Cues

Many see gymnastics merely as an exercise to help the horse figure out how to jump better and/or as a tool to improve the rider's position, but something much bigger comes from them. With practice, horse and rider develop a shared language of subtle cues that strengthens the understanding between them and makes them a more effective team.

Create a gymnastics for your horse. **Here are three different gymnastics you can try, depending on your and your horse's level of education. A horse and rider who have done gymnastics before and are comfortable jumping a course of 2' 9" to 3' should be able to do all three.**

- **All use oxers (wider fences) built from Xs to help point the horse and rider to a natural center and encourage the horse to use his legs correctly.**

- **Note the changes in the exercise from oxer to vertical, making the horse adjust his arc.**

- **Note the variation in length of stride required in Figures B and C.**

Try them all if you're at the appropriate stage of riding — remember to focus on your and your horse's position and form, balance and timing, adjustability, and both of you being straight and centered.

How Is Your Horse's Adjustability?

Ask someone to videotape you and your horse jumping through a gymnastics. Watch the video in slow motion, and consider your horse's arc across the different elements of the gymnastic. Draw his different arcs as he goes through the exercise as though you were creating the Etch A Sketch.

- Can you see how his arc changes among the different elements?

- Does it change from the first time through the gymnastic to the last time?

a. Gymnastics for novice rider or green horse

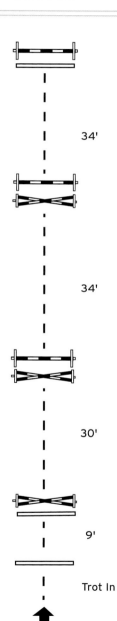

34'

34'

30'

9'

Trot In

b. Gymnastics for advanced rider and/or horse

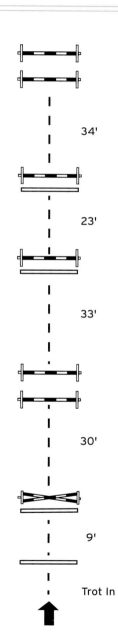

34'

23'

33'

30'

9'

Trot In

c. Gymnastics for advanced rider and/or horse

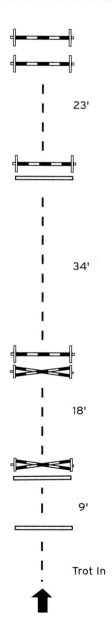

23'

34'

18'

9'

Trot In

The barns and
outdoor arena at
Lionshare Farm,
Greenwich,
Connecticut

7 | Riding the Lines

Track is geometry. Track is your path. Track + Stride = Success.

LINES IN RIDING — we're surrounded by them. As riders we're faced with a broad range of questions that boil down to the common foundation of lines. For example, we face direct, broken, and bending *lines at the jumps*, center and quarter *lines on the flat*, and even *lines on a circle*. But those aren't the only lines that we face. As riders we seek *lines of sight* for a future with horses. We *toe the line* in partnerships with our horse, our families, our trainers, and our friends. And in toeing these lines, we have to open up *lines of communication*.

How can we deal with these different lines, or tracks, as we continue to develop as riders? We've found that by keeping this simple formula in mind, it's easier to manage all the lines we find we need to ride in our lives with horses: Track + Stride = Success.

What do we mean by the line, the track, the path? In this context, it's the road that you'll travel to your destination. If you pick a path and know how to get to your destination, you'll be successful in all areas. Here we focus on picking the right path to each and every jump. And we'll start with geometry.

What does geometry have to do with jumping? Well, geometry is about shapes, and we know shapes are important in riding. Now let's consider a different angle on shapes, one more about geometry and the shape of your ride; a knowledge of geometry can help you find the best track or path to a jump. The geometry is the dotted line between you and the jump.

Terminology

The words "track" and "line" are often used interchangeably in the jumping world. Other terms you might hear are "path," "geometry," and "ride," all of which mean roughly the same thing. "Line" frequently indicates the connection between two jumps, such as a five-stride line, while "track" helps you think more about the actual path in the dirt between the two jumps, which might be a bending line!

THE CONCEPT IN ACTION: Knowledge of Geometry = The Best Track |
Rich Fellers is in the front of the pack when it comes to riding the line needed to win. In addition to his many other talents that make him one of the world's most successful riders, Rich masterfully plans the track he needs to ride and calculates which stride length will be the fastest against the clock. He is often seen putting a curve in a direct line between two jumps so that he can produce a tighter turn on landing over the second jump. He knows his horse and he understands the geometry of the winning track and the range of his mount's stride length, which enables him to regularly dazzle crowds and beat the competition. He confidently answers the questions others don't see the answers to and rides the lines he knows will win.

Direct or Bending: Which Line Will You Ride?

Decide what track you need to ride to win.
Learn to ride the winning track.

A direct line connecting two unrelated fences is straight, so both fences are jumped on an angle.

THERE'S MORE TO A LINE than just the space between fences. Each jump has five parts, which occur in this order:

1. Approach or presentation (your arrival path to the jump)

2. Takeoff (the angle at which your horse leaves the ground)

3. Airborne moment (the path your horse takes in the air)

4. Landing (the exact place and angle at which your horse lands)

5. Ride-away (the line riding away from the jump)

We can't forget about any of these parts when considering a line — they are all part of it. With each line between two jumps, you connect your ride-away from one jump with your approach to the next jump. But that's not all. **Each line also has a point of origin and a point of conclusion** — the places where the line actually starts and ends. All too often a line is thought of just as the space between two jumps, when it actually also includes the approach to the first jump and the ride-away from the final jump.

How Are the Jumps Connected?

Let's talk about terminology for the two main ways in which two jumps are related to one another. There's a **natural connection**, in which the jumps are presented in a way that makes the relationship

THE BOTTOM LINE Learn the different lines that are ridden in hunters, jumpers, and equitation so that you can decide which line/track is the winning one.

between them obvious to the horse. An example is a traditional, straight, five-stride line. But sometimes two jumps are presented with an **unnatural connection**, in which they are set at an angle to one another. In that case it's up to the rider to connect the two jumps for the horse.

In the show world the kinds of lines and the way they're ridden to create the connection may be referred to differently. You'll hear people using such phrases as these:

- A direct five
- A wide six
- Staying in the line
- Staying out in the line
- A slow five
- A normal five
- A big five
- A blind seven
- Using a square turn to do the eight

What do these terms mean? They refer to the track that will be taken or the stride length necessary to ride the line. Let's look at some of the basics about lines to get a better idea of what these phrases refer to. We'll start with the difference between direct and bending lines.

Direct and Bending Lines between Two Fences

Sometimes two fences are set at a slight angle to one another rather than being in a straight line. Anytime you see two fences set with an unnatural connection like this, you should be thinking, "Which line will I ride?" When thinking about riding a line, ask yourself the following questions:

- Where is my point of origin?
- What should the exact location and angle of my horse's takeoff be?
- What should the exact location and angle of my horse's landing be?

The **point of origin** is the place where the line actually starts (see diagrams on pages 132–135). Many riders mistakenly believe that the line starts between the two jumps. *Wrong!* The

Can You Do the S-line Exercise?

One of our favorite exercises is the S line – once you've mastered it, you are ready to jump today's courses. It has many, many variations to challenge yourself and your horse. It's a wonderful exercise for you to practice at home.

- First do the exercise with bending lines. Follow the blue line in lining up your horse's feet with the line.

- When you've mastered the bending lines, try the direct line. The red line represents where you want your horse to be for the direct line.

This exercise will tell the truth – whether or not you've got it! If not, keep practicing . . . it will come!

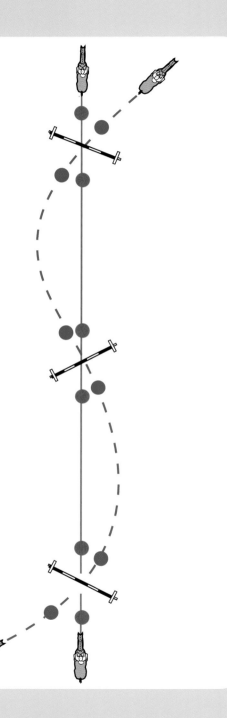

line starts where you leave the track to approach the fence. As you can see in the diagram on page 132, lines A, B, and C have very different points of origin.

The point of origin affects every aspect of your jump. Your line will be successful if you pick the appropriate point of origin; you can find it by locating the spot that begins the straight line to the line you want to ride. The best point of origin is the one that gives your horse a clear approach to the fence and line you're planning to execute.

What Line for What Ride?

So how do you know which line to ride when? Let's look a little more closely at how each type of line might help you, both with actual jumping and when it comes to judging, as well as considering what to remember when riding each one.

Bending Line

Pluses: Flows forward, looks smooth, demonstrates advanced skill level.

Key Point: Stick with your plan. It's easy to put more bend into a line than you planned on, which will throw your stride count off.

Remember: Try to have your horse land on the lead corresponding to the direction you're bending. There's nothing more beautiful than landing on the correct leg and not having to change your lead in the middle of the line.

Direct Line

Pluses: Faster; shows off rider precision and commitment; can convey horse and rider confidence and ability.

Key Point: Jumping fences on angles can be intimidating and difficult for some horses and riders — be sure to stick to your plan.

Remember: Deviating even slightly from the direct line will increase the distance between the two jumps and possibly compromise your plan for stride count.

try this

Set three poles on the ground as shown on page 130 for the S-line exercise. Walk the two lines to determine where each of the lines pictured in the diagram are. On foot "canter" the line yourself. Determine which line you'll ride each time and then stick to it.

When you're sure of where the lines are and how it feels to canter each one, try it on a horse. Have someone videotape you and see if you can guess which line you were riding. If it's clear, great job; if you can't tell, try again!

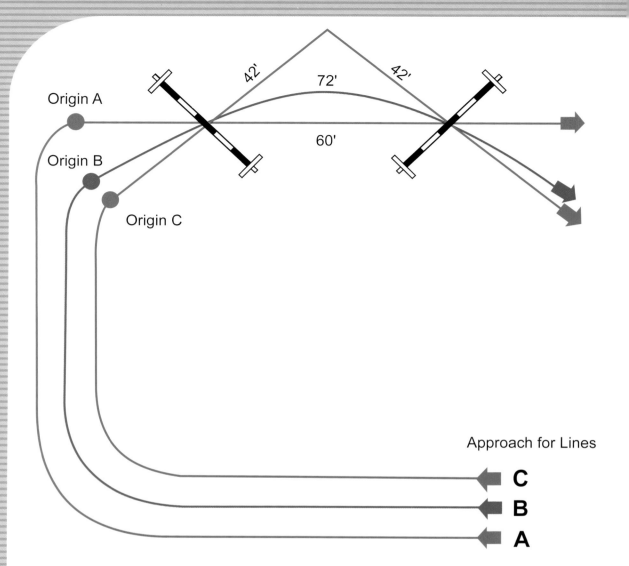

Origin A

Origin B

Origin C

42'

72'

42'

60'

Approach for Lines

C

B

A

With any series of jumps, you can choose from several different lines.

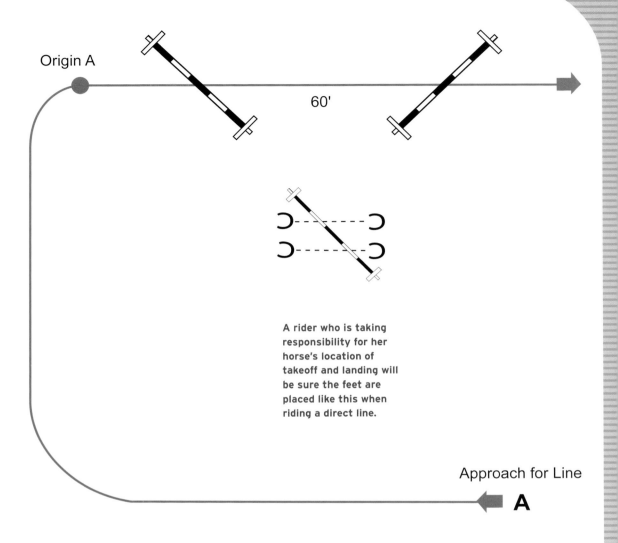

Origin A

60'

A rider who is taking
responsibility for her
horse's location of
takeoff and landing will
be sure the feet are
placed like this when
riding a direct line.

Approach for Line

A

KEEP IT DIRECT

Line A involves riding to both fences with a perfectly straight line through the two fences (although we hope you go over the fences, rather than through them!). As you can see from the diagram, it's impossible to ride a perfectly straight line without jumping each fence on an angle; that is, rather than having your horse perpendicular to the fence when jumping, your horse's body and the jump will be more like an X from a bird's-eye view. This is called riding a direct line. We know that the shortest distance between two points is a straight line, so the direct line shown above will ride in four strides.

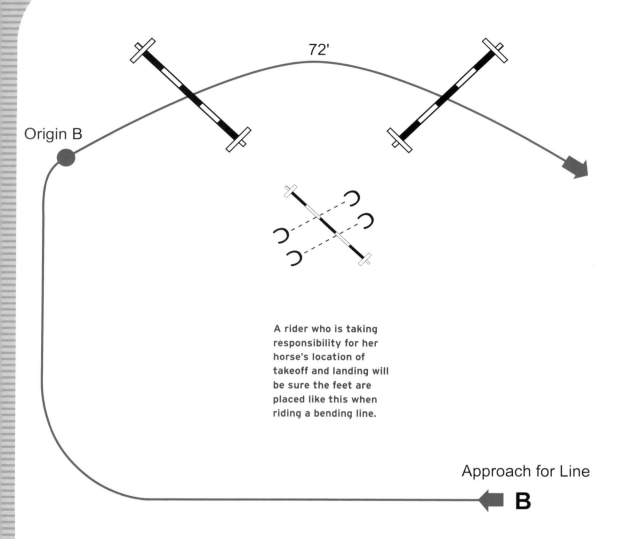

72'

Origin B

A rider who is taking
responsibility for her
horse's location of
takeoff and landing will
be sure the feet are
placed like this when
riding a bending line.

Approach for Line

B

BEND THAT BABY

Line B is a "bending line." Here your track follows a curved path. In between the jumps you'll ride a soft curve from fence 1 to fence 2. This ride should work nicely in five strides in a bending line. For the most part the two fences will be jumped straight, meaning that the horse's body will be perpendicular to the jump, like a T.

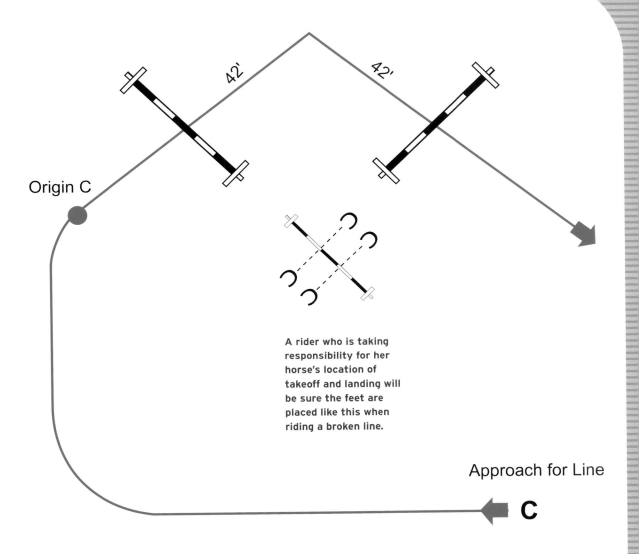

Origin C

42'   42'

A rider who is taking
responsibility for her
horse's location of
takeoff and landing will
be sure the feet are
placed like this when
riding a broken line.

Approach for Line

C

HOW MUCH BEND?

With this line both fences are also jumped straight on, with the horse's body perpendicular to the jump. The difference is that the smooth line curves, or bows, out farther — almost to the point of being a gentle corner.

With this kind of line, it's important to ride as smoothly as the softer flex in line B so the turn isn't too abrupt. A well-ridden line with a bigger bow takes careful execution. A half-halt at the point of the turn lets your horse know that it's time to shift his weight back and turn slightly.

Because you're using more space to create it, Line C will typically require one more stride than the previous example. In this case it would be a six-stride line. Depending on the location of the fences, the number of strides may be equal on each part of the line (for example, three strides and three strides), or they may not.

Direct Line

Here the rider is executing a direct straight line between these two unrelated fences. Note the angle at which the horse arrives and rides away from each jump.

Bending Line

This rider has chosen a bending or broken line. In this case, the arrival angle to each jump is perpendicular to the center of the jump.

Do the Math and See in the Moment

When walking a course, see and feel where you are in a line so that you can let go of it and ride what you see. Blend what you see with what you know you walked.

WHEN WALKING A COURSE or reading a course diagram at a show, how do you know how many strides there are between the fences? It helps to remember a couple of key things:

An average horse's stride is 12 feet long. That means that one canter stride covers 12 feet of ground.

The takeoff and landing equals one stride on average, or about 6 feet on each side of the jump. So: Landing (6 feet) + takeoff (6 feet) = a full canter stride (12 feet)

Let's do some simple math to be sure we understand. In the diagram on the next page, the direct line, Line A, measures 60 feet between fence 1 and fence 2. Here's how to figure out the number of strides a horse will take in Line A:

- Subtract 6 feet for the landing after fence 1 and another 6 feet for the takeoff at fence 2: 60 − 12 = 48 feet

- Divide the remaining number by 12 (the length of a stride): 48 ÷ 12 = 4 strides

THE BOTTOM LINE Learning to calculate the strides and distances between jumps is important, but seeing the ride in the moment is also key.

Familiarize yourself with the typical 12-foot distances in lines so when you see them on a course map you will be able to calculate the number of strides that footage represents.

Walking an Actual Line

Imagine that there is no course diagram and you're on your own to figure out how many strides there are between two jumps. That's what **walking a course** means. The easiest way to figure out the strides is to use your own stride, typically about 3 feet long. That means that four human strides equal one horse stride. Here's how you walk the distances and determine the number of strides yourself:

1. Stand on the back side of fence 1 with your heel on the back side of the ground line (the back side is in between the two jumps), and take two 3-foot steps. That's the landing.

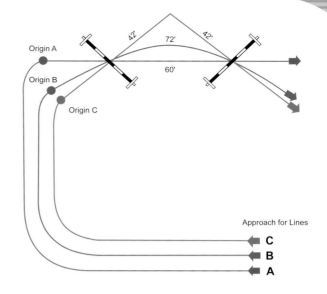

Origin A

Origin B

Origin C

42'
72'
42'
60'

Approach for Lines

C
B
A

2. Count off the remaining distance in 3-foot steps: "One, two, three, one; one, two, three, two; one, two, three, three; one, two, three, four; one, two."

Those last two are the takeoff, so you know that this line would ride in four strides. If you only got one last step instead of two, then you know it's a shorter four-stride because it's 3 feet shorter than a normal four.

Fences are set specific distances apart on each course. In the United States distances are set in feet; other countries use meters (in this case 42 feet [13 m]).

TYPICAL DISTANCES ON A COURSE

Feet in line	Number of 12-foot strides (after landing and takeoff are accounted for)
36 feet	Two strides
48 feet	Three strides
60 feet	Four strides
72 feet	Five strides
84 feet	Six strides
96 feet	Seven strides

If you got three last steps, then you know it's a really forward four because it's 3 feet longer than a normal four.

Lines and Combinations Are Different!

As discussed above, regular lines are typically walked in terms of strides. The strides are stepped off, and if you end up shorter or longer at the second jump, you adjust the last strides you counted up to accordingly (either short or long, depending on how much room is left for the takeoff of the second jump).

Combinations, or jumps that are two or three strides apart, are walked from the standard of jump A to the standard of jump B. They're walked in 3-foot steps so the exact footage is known.

Make sure you **know the typical distance for a combination**, so that when you're stepping one off and measuring it you know how it will ride relative to the typical distance (see chart below). Note that most riders school tighter combination distances at home than they face at a show. This is because it is harder to successfully jump a tight combination than a normal or long one. In general, jumping short combinations helps the horse jump with better technique using the hind end.

Seeing Is Understanding

Measuring a distance on the ground makes sense, but what do people

DISTANCES BETWEEN COMBINATIONS

Typical Combination Distances, Show Ring	
Hunter, one-stride	25' 6"
Hunter, two-stride	36' 6"
Jumper, normal one-stride	25' 6"
Jumper, short one-stride	24' 6"
Jumper, normal two-stride	35' 6"
Jumper, short two-stride	34' 6"
Typical Combination Distances, Training at Home (varies by type of training, age and ability of horse, etc.)	
Hunter, one-stride	24' 6"
Hunter, two-stride	35'
Jumper, one-stride	24'
Jumper, two-stride	34'

mean when they talk about "seeing the distance" and "feeling the strides" and "delivering the ride"? In the world of jumping, **"seeing" is understanding what is happening at each moment**. Seeing is knowing where you and your horse are relative to the plan, and relative to the jump, at all times. It means knowing if . . .

- the geometry you planned out is working the way you thought it would
- your horse's body is where it should be when it should be
- you have the room to continue at your current pace and still ride the number of strides you have left in the plan

While knowing the mathematical distances and knowing the number of strides a line walked in are key,

It's Complicated

Riding involves a complex kind of knowing. It's not just knowing the facts from looking at the course diagram and walking the course before you get on your horse. It's also about knowing whether the ride looks and feels as though it's going according to your plan after you get on. And knowing is also being able to adjust as necessary.

it's also important not to rely totally on that information. Rather, you must also **develop your sight** when riding and keep asking yourself, "Does my plan match what I'm seeing in the moment?"

spotcheck

Have You Mastered the 3-foot Step?

How do you know if you're taking a 3-foot step? It's easy! Just lay a 12-foot jump pole on the ground. Starting at one end, practice walking next to the pole over and over until you can take four evenly spaced steps every time.

When you have that down, put two pieces of masking tape 24 feet apart and see if you can mark off 8 even steps in between the two. If you can, then you've got it, and you're ready to walk a real course!

THE CONCEPT IN ACTION: Walking versus Seeing | Peter (shown above on Legato) tells this story about the Friday Grand Prix at the Monterey Five-Star at La Silla in 1995:

Linda Allen designed the course, and it was tough. After Aachen, this was the best show in the world at the time. In those days the U.S. riders didn't compete against the Europeans very often, so we were excited. There were ten of us representing the team. We all walked the first line and discovered that it walked a forward eight strides. We thought that in the jump-off we could all do it in seven to win. Hugo Simon went first. He galloped in and took that first line in *six* strides!

We'd had a plan based on what we walked. But wow — now we saw something different from what we'd walked. The incredible range of the equine stride taught us that how the line rides is more important than how it walks. I'll never forget it: Six strides that walked eight! But we watched and learned and followed suit. We did the six and won.

Ride the Body for the Best Track

Our job as riders is to channel the horse's energy from back to front, with our legs, not our hands.

MANY OF US WERE taught in our first riding lessons to use our legs to make the horse go and our hands to make him stop. It can be difficult to forget those early lessons, but to ride effectively, you may have to unlearn them.

Even though we know that our horse's action has to come from behind, we automatically turn to our hands for just about every type of correction. If we're crooked, we steer straight. If we're fast, we pull to slow down. It makes sense, because we use our hands instinctively for just about everything we do on a daily basis. We use them to reach and grasp, push and pull, open and close, type and drive, and so on. We don't do a whole lot with our legs except walk, run, and stand!

So why wouldn't we want to use our hands a lot of the time when riding horses? We can't really help it, without lots of careful thinking about the issue.

Back to the Engine

In chapter 2 we talked about the fact that the horse is a rear-engined animal. All **the horse's power and energy come from the hind end**, and that power must be told to go somewhere. If it's not told where to go, it may go straight through the body, or it may not. It's our job as riders to channel that energy by riding the body of the horse from back to front.

Always push your horse to the desired track from back to front; don't pull him onto it.

THE BOTTOM LINE To ride your chosen track successfully, you must guide your horse's body, not his head. Use both legs and both reins, not just your hands!

Now let's connect how that rear engine relates to the track we've been discussing. To get from point A to point B, **the horse's entire body must be on the track**, the path, the geometry that we need to ride. And to make that happen you need to shift your thinking from "the legs say go, hands steer and stop" to a "ride the body" view of how to ride your horse. What does that feel like?

Riding the body suggests **a different way of approaching your jumping**. It means that when you feel your horse pull on the bit, you close your leg

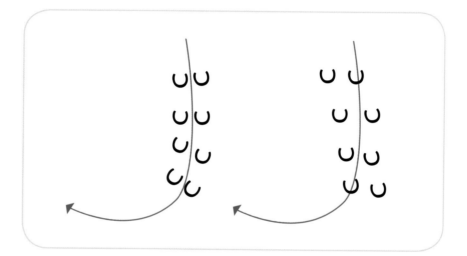

Consider two horses cantering on the right lead to a jump. The horse on the right is not tracking on the path the rider has set. You can see his hind footprints are to the inside, or the right, of his front footprints. The horse on the left, however, is tracking correctly on the chosen path. His hind footprints are following directly behind the front footprints.

What are the consequences for each of these horses? The horse on the left is going to be straight and will stay on the desired track. The horse on the right is going to lose momentum – his flow, his stride, and his distance – because his energy is drifting outside the track to the left. The energy from the hind legs that are not on the track is being lost through the body that is also not on the track.

and fix that feeling from the back of the horse rather than from the front by pulling on the reins. It means that when you come around a corner to your fence, you not only think about where you're going and what's in front of you, but you also think in-tensely about what your horse's hind feet are doing. **What is his body doing?** If the horse is "behind you" (not moving forward and bringing his hind end underneath himself) as you come out of a turn to a jump, you're in trouble.

Riding the body enables you to ride your track correctly.

Are You Riding the Body?

It takes careful concentration to change your habits, but once you do it, it becomes second nature. Try this the next time you ride:

- Hook your thumbs together while you hold the reins.

- Work your horse as usual, riding some circles and serpentines.

- When you are tempted to pull or move your hands to straighten the horse, think about riding the body instead and shift your upper body weight back while closing your legs.

The hands complement what the legs and seat tell the horse to do. Let your weight distribution help you. It's all about breaking the habit we all have of using our hands first. Riding the body involves thinking about what's behind your saddle and telling the body what to do with your legs and seat, first and foremost.

IS THE BODY ON THE TRACK? One way to find out if you're riding the body on the geometry you've chosen is to ride in a freshly dragged arena. Plan a specific shape and ride it once, then study your horse's footprints. Do they look like those of the horse on the left or those of the one on the right on page 144?

Ride several different shapes at the walk, trot, and canter. And ride a halt, too. See if you can ride the body through all the shapes, transitions, and gaits. Let the footprints tell the truth.

Dancing Lions
fence, 2008
Beijing Olympics

8 | The Building Blocks of Today's Courses

Today's courses are far more technical and therefore more difficult than ever before.

TODAY'S COURSES REQUIRE a sophisticated understanding of show jumping. They require that you do your homework, understand the questions asked by a given course, and know how to answer them.

Building blocks: To succeed in any sport, it's important to understand the building blocks that equal success in that sport — what they are, how to establish them, what they feel like, how you put them together for success.

Here we consider three different building blocks for successfully jumping in competition:

- Taking a piece-by-piece approach
- Mastering the prime jumping questions
- "Making it work" at each jump

Isolate the Pieces and Take Them One at a Time

Break the course down into simple pieces that you can master with confidence.

Prepare your horse's balance, stride, and track to answer the whole course question. Then jump each jump, keeping in mind its relation to the whole question.

MASTERING TODAY'S courses requires both a clear understanding of the different pieces that make up each course and the ability to execute those pieces with confidence. The best advice is to identify the individual pieces of the course, ride each part well, and string those good rides together.

This means that when you first look at a course you try to identify the natural pieces that it breaks down into. You can't account for enough detail if you think about that entire ride all at once. Rather, you **take the questions posed by each jump** or natural unit of the course as separate pieces. So far we've talked about lines, corners, the right track, reset-ting, the different phases of the jump itself. There are a lot of parts for every jump. It can be overwhelming on a course with 8 to 14 jumps.

Is that TMI? If you try to think about it all at the same time, yes, it is Too Much Information. But if you break it down, the answer is no. When you break the course into simple jump-able parts, pieces, or questions, you can process it and ride it success-fully. Think of identifying the pieces, the questions, that you *know* you can answer. By breaking the course down, you can **master it by jumping each piece correctly** because those are the pieces you've practiced at home or experienced in previous competitions.

THE BOTTOM LINE Shift your mind-set from jumping a whole course to jumping pieces of a course. This helps you clearly understand and execute each piece more successfully.

But how do we do that? Here's one suggestion: Examine the whole course on paper (either the posted course diagram or your own sketch), looking at the sequence of the jumps, the turns, and so on. All courses tend to have a natural breakdown, and most break into three to six simple pieces.

Try to take in the overall feeling of the whole course. **Sense the flow:** right, right, left, straight, roll back, and so forth. Then identify the natural pieces that make sense: a one-stride to a two-stride in a line, a single jump, an S line, fences five-six-seven, the rollback on a single, a combination, the last line.

Identify the Pieces

Jumping is a process; it's not a moment in time. In general you don't want just to identify trouble spots and ride from one trouble spot to another. Identify pieces you can remember, understand, and execute. In identifying the natural pieces that make sense, we're breaking down the course into **the prime jumping questions:** the direct and bending lines we covered in chapter 7, the type of jump, the number of strides between elements, and so on.

An Example

Suppose you're entering a triple combination — a tight one-stride to a forward two. You might be tempted to gallop in strong to make the forward out. But you'll have trouble jumping the first tight part of the triple if you gallop in thinking about the forward two.

You have to jump the A element slowly, to let your horse land shallow and have room to jump the B element, *then* move up to the C element. You can't enter the combination thinking only of the long distance from B to C.

You must assess and ride each jumping question within the larger challenge of answering a sequence of jumping questions. Set the stage with your stride length, track, and balance, then let your horse take the time to jump the individual jumps within the sequence.

When you land, assess, react, and execute the rest of the line. You're always managing the performance, the stride, the track, and the jumping effort in relationship to the whole course question.

As each element comes up, you have to **jump that particular jump.** But not until you're faced with it.

Rolex FEI World Cup Leipzig 2011

Class No.: 3
World Cup III Round 1
Competition over two
rounds
Sunday, May 01, 2011
Start: 15:30

Table: A
National RG:
FEI RG / Art. 659.1.2.7
Height: 1.60m

Speed: 350 m/min
Length: 440 m
T. allowed: 76 sec
T. limit: 152 sec

Obstacles: 12
Efforts: 15

Reproduced from
original course map designed by
Frank Rothenberger

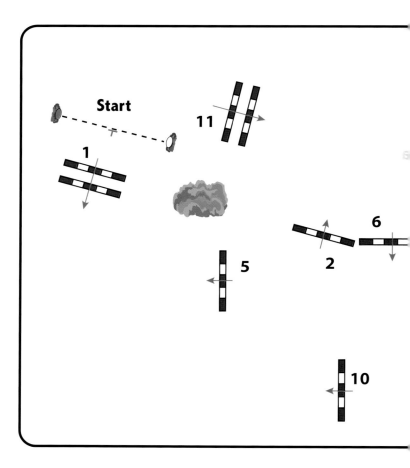

Though at first it takes very focused concentration to identify the prime jumping questions, as you ride more courses, the pieces begin to present themselves to you. It's like a word search — when you first look at one, you see a bunch of letters and not the words. But over time you become better at seeing the words. With practice your brain will learn to see the pieces, and you'll learn to **break a course into the prime jumping questions** the minute you look at it.

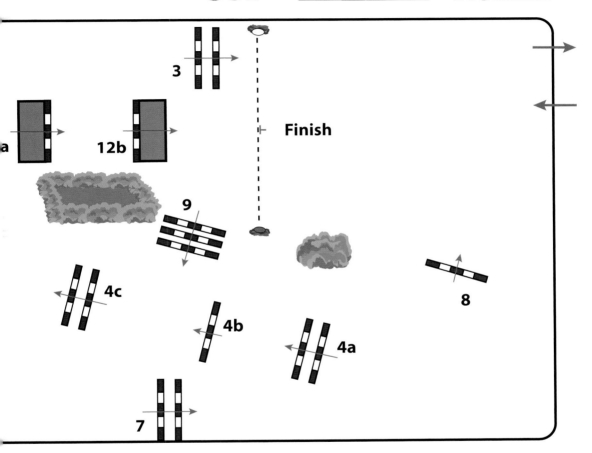

3

a   12b

9

4c

4b

4a

8

7

Finish

ISOLATING THE PIECES: 2011 WORLD CUP FINAL, LEIPZIG, GERMANY

The World Cup Final course shown above can be broken down into jumpable pieces just
like any other course. In fact, the bigger the event, the more important it is to compartmentalize the course in
order to master it. Here is how I break down this course:

Entrance: ride past 4a,b,c, 5, and 12, then reset ▪ Start: single jump #1; broken line #2 to # 3 ▪
triple combination #4a,b,c to #5 ▪ (make time) bending line to bending line #6 to #7 to #8 ▪ rollback on
broken line #9 to #10 ▪ direct line to double combination #11 to #12a & 12b. Each of these pieces
are connected to each other by riding a neat track at the necessary rhythm to be under the time allowed.

Identify the Prime Jumping Questions

We can remember and jump a complex course by breaking it down into simple pieces.

THE ELEMENTS OF TODAY'S jumping courses are put together in new ways to continue the increasing trend of technicality and difficulty. We've identified a number of typical questions you'll find in just about any show jumping, hunter, or equitation course. While many of them used to be found only in show jumping (e.g., rollbacks, triple combinations), today you'll find them across *any* of the high-performance jumping arenas.

Are these questions I should be asking myself? The answer is no. **By "questions" we mean the elements of a typical course** that will test your riding ability and your horse's experience. Each of the prime jumping questions requires a very specific answer by both horse and rider.

They're questions that are designed to examine different aspects of a complete jumping and training education, including your ability to lengthen and shorten, to turn, to be straight, to adjust, and to be bold. Here are many of them:

- Direct line
- Bending line
- S line
- Line to a line
  - Long to long
  - Long to short
  - Short to long
  - Short to short
- Rollback (270 degrees)
- Water jump
  - Liverpool and ditch
- Spooky (full) jump

THE BOTTOM LINE If you can identify the types of jumping questions found in today's hunters, equitation, and jumper courses, you can effectively and consistently put in a competitive performance.

- Airy jump

- Skinny (narrow) jump

- Combinations (doubles and triples)
    Short to long
    Long to short

- Spread to vertical/
  vertical in-and-out

- Half-strided line

- Single jump

Each of these questions comes with its own challenges. For example, big water jumps require a specific ride by a well-schooled horse and rider. In fact, there has a been a great deal of debate and discussion about water jumps lately in the show jumping world, with the consensus being that they aren't enough of a part of the courses juniors and amateurs typically face. When big waters show up as part of a finals course,

the riders often don't have the experience or the education to ride them.

Our point here is to make you aware of a number of different questions that you will typically see in a show ring, regardless of your discipline. You can **take four steps to prepare yourself** to tackle them at your next show.

- Learn what each question looks like

- Recognize the questions when they are part of a course

- Understand the characteristic challenges and demands of each question

- Practice jumping the questions at home so you can answer them in competition

try this

Find a horse show course to review online or in person. **Break the course down by the list of questions: How many of them are used? Not used? Which questions seem to pose the most problems for the horses? Which ones the least?**

Once you've mastered the practice above, try explaining the different questions to a local Pony Club or 4-H group. **Set up small versions of each of the questions, and have a "horseless"**

horse show; watch how differently kids use their bodies over each one. For example, note how they use their bodies to lean back and do the rollback.

Back at your barn and with your trainer, try one or more of them out with your horse. **Try to picture how the balance needs to change for the different types of jumps. For example, are you helping your horse roll back by leaning back behind the vertical?**

The Prime Jumping Questions Defined*

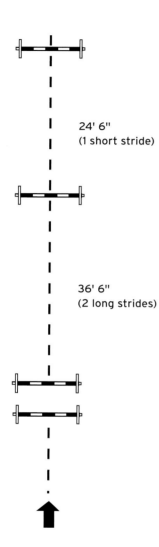

24' 6"
(1 short stride)

36' 6"
(2 long strides)

TRIPLE COMBINATION
(long to short) Three fences set in a straight line with related distances of either one or two strides; this combination is two long strides to one short one.

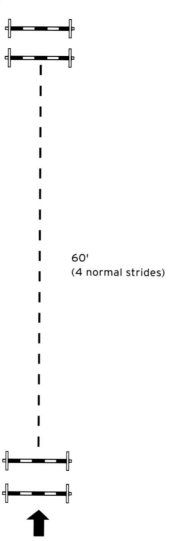

60'
(4 normal strides)

DIRECT LINE
Two fences related to one another in a straight line

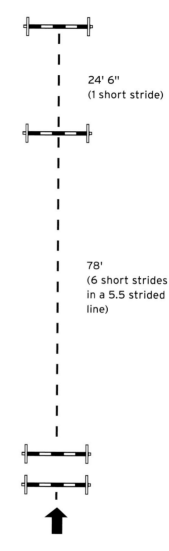

24' 6"
(1 short stride)

78'
(6 short strides in a 5.5 strided line)

SPREAD TO TIGHT VERTICAL/VERTICAL IN-AND-OUT
This is a classic show jumping question: five and a half strides to a very short vertical/vertical in-and-out; six strides are needed to make that short single stride.

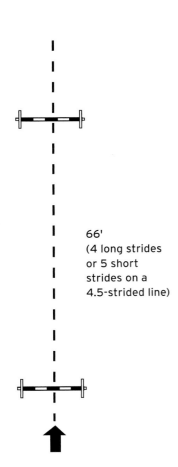

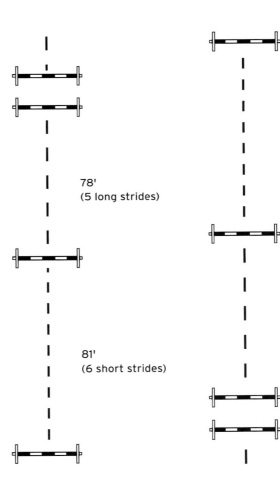

66'
(4 long strides
or 5 short
strides on a
4.5-strided line)

78'
(5 long strides)

81'
(6 short strides)

81'
(6 short strides)

78'
(5 long strides)

**HALF-STRIDED
LINE**
A line set so that the
related distance isn't
obvious because it is
on the half stride.
You could make either
four or five strides.

SHORT TO LONG
This line requires
six short strides to
five long ones.

LONG TO SHORT
Here the five long
strides come before
the short six to the
next fence.

* Distances in a combination ride differently than distances in a line;
see chart on page 140.

The Prime Jumping Questions Defined, continued

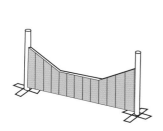

SINGLE JUMP
A jump that
stands by itself
on the course

AIRY JUMP
A jump with little,
if any, filler material,
making it look insub-
stantial, which can
make it more difficult
for the horse to judge
the top rail

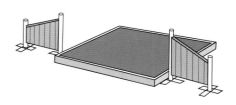

WATER JUMP
A 10-foot or larger
water obstacle,
sometimes
with a rail and a
takeoff box

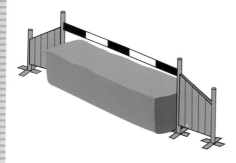

**SPOOKY
(FULL) JUMP**
A jump with a
great deal of filler,
making it look
more intimidating
to the horse

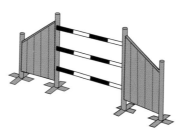

SKINNY JUMP
A narrow jump, usu-
ally 10 feet or less
in width, that can
be built of either
lightweight or solid
material

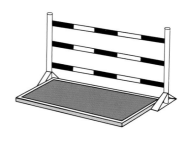

**LIVERPOOLS
AND DITCHES**
A liverpool is a small
water jump up to 6
feet across; a ditch
is a trench dug under
the fence. Both have
an obstacle in front,
over, or behind.

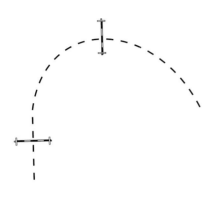

BENDING (BROKEN) LINE
Two fences not clearly related to one
another and not in a straight line

S LINE
A series of three fences set along
an S-shaped pattern

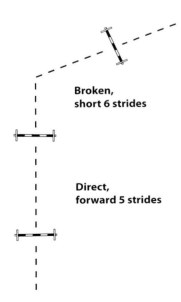

**Broken,
short 6 strides**

**Direct,
forward 5 strides**

LINE TO A LINE
Two different direct lines
in sequential order

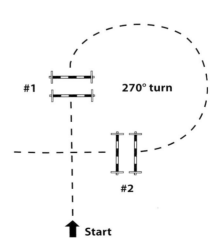

#1

270° turn

#2

Start

ROLLBACKS (270 DEGREES)
Two fences with a 270-degree turn
connecting them

Ride the Prime Jumping Questions

Each of today's prime jumping questions requires a specific answer, or ride, from horse and rider.

NOW WE COME to the answers that each of the prime jumping questions requires from both horse and rider. Let's think about those questions and answers together, so that when you're faced with any of these questions in the show ring, you'll not only recognize them but will also know how to answer them.

A Direct Line

Q. Can the rider keep a chute with her legs and keep the horse straight on the correct track?

A. The key to succeeding with direct lines is to commit to the straight track, use your legs as a chute, and take responsibility for making sure your horse's feet take off and land on the direct line. See chapter 7 for more on direct lines.

A Bending or Broken Line

Q. Can the rider show the horse where to go next and make two unrelated fences related?

A. Identify a bending line specifically, commit to that track, and be sure to guide your horse with your eyes, both legs, and both reins. Drifting in or bulging out relative to the correct track will result in a mistake at the next jump.

An S Line

Q. Can the rider select the option that best shows her and her horse's strengths?

THE BOTTOM LINE Learn the inherent question being asked by each type of fence, and learn how to answer those questions.

A. Be sure to select the line you know you and your horse can execute most effectively.

A Line to a Line

Q. Can horse and rider reset between the two lines to successfully navigate the second one?

A. Focus carefully, remember the related distances, and execute the half-halt in just the right place so you can adjust accordingly. If the lines are long ones, make sure your horse does not become too strung out from one line to the next.

A Rollback (270 Degrees)

Q. How accurately can the rider communicate with her horse through the turn, since the horse will have no idea where he's going?

A. Use your eyes and outside aids. Upon landing over the first jump, your eyes must be intensely focused on the second fence to indicate the turn and communicate to your horse where you are going. The inside leg should block the inside shoulder to produce the correct lead, which will eliminate the need for a lead change. Finally, the outside leg should drive the horse's body through the turn, putting his focus on the second jump.

Water jump at the individual finals at the 2008 Beijing Olympics

A Water Jump

Q. Is the horse brave, scopey, and conscientious enough to clear the obstacle?

A. This type of jump requires a mix of scope (the ability to jump wide), conscientiousness (the desire not to step in the water), and bravery (the willingness to jump it at all) from your horse. You need to be sure he has an open stride and that he arrives at the jump close to the takeoff box so he has the opportunity to clear the tape.

Liverpools and Ditches

Q. Are horse and rider capable of being brave and careful while adjusting to a difficult task?

A. To jump natural obstacles in the ring you should enter prepared: Practice them at home or at a nearby facility. If you and your horse are familiar with these types of jumps, you will have no problem.

Spooky (full) jump at
Aachen, Germany

Airy (skinny) jump
at the 2008 Beijing Olympics

A Spooky (Full) Jump

Q. **Are horse and rider brave enough to maintain the balance needed for the scope that these full fences often require?**

A. Designed as much to spook riders as horses, these jumps are mentally challenging, but are actually physically inviting in their shape and fullness. The key to conquering these types of jumps is to not hesitate at all; offer your horse a solid, support-ive ride that indicates you are sure it's fine to jump the spooky fence.

Short to Long

Q. **Can horse and rider adjust between fences and still be accurate?**

A. Enter the first part of the line with a more collected horse, allow-ing the horse to jump quietly in for the short distance. Upon landing ask for and obtain a longer length of step to successfully make the longer distance more comfortable and fence 3 a success.

An Airy or Skinny (Narrow) Jump

Q. **How careful is the horse going over a lightweight or narrow-looking fence that might invite him to run out or rub the top rail?**

A. Be sure your horse is not flat in his approach; you'll need a smooth and consistent connection arriving at the jump to focus him for a good effort.

Long to Short

Q. **Can horse and rider adjust between fences and still be accurate?**

A. Be sure the horse is entering the line with enough pace to master the long distance but not be too flat to collect for the shorter stride required from fence 2 to fence 3. The key to this type of question is impulsion and careful execution of timing in asking for the change in balance and stride from your horse.

Know how
to answer
today's prime
jumping
questions.

Triple combination at the 2008
Beijing Olympics

Combinations (Doubles and Triples)

Q. **Can horse and rider react with adjustability, accuracy, and athleticism?**

A. Doing your homework and training on combinations at home is essential to jumping them successfully in the show ring. Training through gymnastics provides a great base of understanding for horse and rider.

A Spread to a Vertical/Vertical In-and-Out

Q. **Can the rider adjust both stride and balance?**

A. The oxer is likely to cause horse to get strong and strung out, while the vertical-to-vertical in-and-out requires a short stride and composed balance. This is a fundamental competition question. Hours of flatwork practicing extension and collection provide the key to jumping this line successfully.

A Half-strided Line

Q. **Can the rider commit to a ride and not waver midway, compromising her distance and balance at the second fence?**

A. Consider what is best for your horse's natural way of going, then stick with the decision that builds on his strengths. It is also important to know where you are at all times inside the line, so you can accurately gauge if your plan and stride are sufficiently answering the question.

A Single Jump

Q. **Can horse and rider maintain a consistent and appropriate pace down to a single fence?**

A. A single jump is all about maintaining smoothness and composure. In the jumper ring, you need to concentrate on putting your horse back together. The key to answering this question is to focus on riding the body of the horse in a consistent rhythm straight along the desired track at an appropriate pace. The hardest thing about jumping a single jump is remaining patient with your eye!

EYES ON THE PRIZE:

Showing and Competing

Mark Leone
on Great
American at
the Washington
International
Horse Show,
2012

9 Putting It All Together in the Ring

When you're at home, pretend you're in the show ring. When you're in the show ring, pretend you're at home.

WE'VE GONE OVER flatwork and how the flatwork sets the stage for us to be able to answer most jumping questions. We've talked about and identified the core jumping training exercises that enable you to answer any and all competition jumping questions. We've shown that all competition courses are broken down into the same questions in different arenas with different footing. Now it's time to put you in the show ring and put it all together.

We can talk on and on about mastering a little piece at a time, but when it comes down to keeping your mind clear and focused to execute an entire course, things are more complicated. So what's the secret to putting all the pieces together into a coherent, lovely, "big picture' round? There are a few simple steps:

- Trust your homework
- Create déjà vu moments
- Warm up and ace the test!

We told you it was simple, but it's not always easy! In this chapter we explore these steps to success on the course.

Practice, Practice, Practice, Then Trust Your Homework

You've put in the time, you've practiced the flatwork, you've identified the questions. Now trust your homework.

Trust the experience that doing your homework gives you.

WHEN PUTTING everything together in the show ring for a beautiful ride, you have to first think about what homework you've done that helps forge the connections between the pieces. What are the connecting mechanisms you've practiced?

- **LOOK.** Look ahead to the next jump.

- **RESET.** If you need to, reset your horse's balance and stride.

- **EXECUTE.** You're prepared; now jump the next question.

You can do all these things because you've done your homework.

One thing, though — in trusting your homework, it's a given that you've *done* your homework. You need to **practice not only the different pieces but also entire courses** so you can become good at managing yourself and your horse over a complete course.

The Value of Homework

George Morris always says, "It's not that practice makes perfect; it's *perfect* practice that makes perfect." We couldn't agree more. While it can be overwhelming to think about making all your practices perfect, it's about a mind-set. It's about **commitment**, as we discussed in chapter 5. You can trust your homework when putting things all together because regular practice does several things:

THE BOTTOM LINE When you understand the role of focused practice in developing your riding, you will begin to trust your homework as you put the pieces together in the show ring.

- It helps your muscles develop a memory about how to respond to different situations.

- It builds "scripts" in your brain that eventually will become completely automatic responses.

- It provides the opportunity to have successes that build your confidence.

- It gives you a foundation to rely on when faced with a new situation.

In a perfect world you could practice as much as you'd like. But let's be realistic: You don't live in a perfect world, and your attention is devoted to things in your life other than riding. And that's okay. You also need to consider your horse. He cannot physically endure all the practice sessions you may want or need.

But while acknowledging that you need to practice so you trust your homework, you also need to be realistic. You need to set goals and identify how you're going to reach them. It's important to consider the practice requirements of reaching those goals and how they fit into your daily routine. Practice as much as you can, but **be realistic** with yourself and your trainer.

Mind over Matter
There's another kind of mind-set that's necessary for putting it all together. That mind-set involves composure and patience: **Composure** so you can focus. **Patience** so you don't let your horse (or yourself) build within a course as you put the pieces together.

Putting it all together requires not only that you trust your homework but that you stay composed and patient under the pressure that comes from putting it all together. You have to **trust that you are prepared** and **have the mind-set to focus** throughout the entire course. It's about perseverance and mind over matter!

10,000 Hours of Practice?!

Research shows that it takes 10,000 hours of focused practice to develop a truly expert ability or "automatic pilot" for a complicated activity. Ten thousand hours – that's a lot of practice. Riding an hour a day, 5 days a week equals 260 hours a year. At that rate you'd have to ride for 38 years to hit the 10,000-hour mark – wow. That's a lot of time in the saddle!

You can do it right because you have done the homework, you know how it should feel, and you know what to do!

try this

Here's an effective way to develop your ability to master the whole course. This exercise allows you to focus on putting it all together piece by piece, with the circles as places to remind you to reset the balance and stride of your horse as you patiently put the course together.

- Set a basic six-jump course at home.

- Take it piece by piece.

- Ride down a line and circle at the end.

- Ride down the next line and circle.

- Ride down the last line and circle.

Repeat the exercise until your course, including the circles, is consistent in pace, balance, stride length, and rhythm.

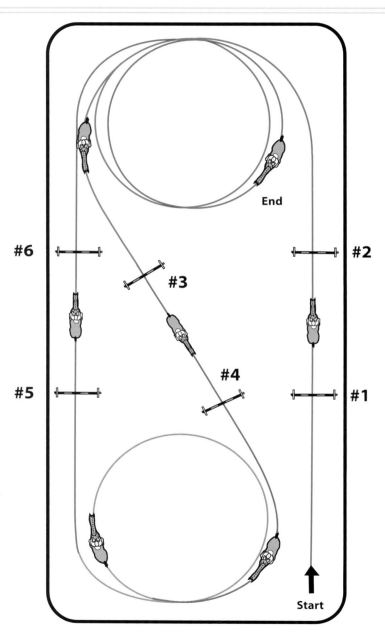

Create Déjà Vu Moments

Get inside the course designer's mind.
Know what he or she is asking for.

IN CHAPTER 8 we covered the prime jumping questions of today's courses. We talked about how it's important to recognize each question and to learn the unique requirements of riding each one. **What about the overall picture?** The way the different elements are put together at different shows? For different classes? By different course designers?

Now let's talk about taking that basic knowledge and sensing the next level of questions the course designer is asking riders to solve:

- Related and unrelated fences

- Distances

- Solid obstacles and natural obstacles

- Scopeyness

- Accuracy

- Rideability

- Technicality

The ability to recognize these questions, to get inside the course designer's mind, separates winning riders from the rest of the pack.

How Do I Do That?
Read. Watch. Ask. Pay attention. **Learn who the course designer is for every show.** It's in the front of the prize list. Look at the types of courses at that show. What kinds of questions are being asked? Read magazine or online articles about course designers so you can learn what they were trying to accomplish with their designs. **Study course maps,** even when you're not riding in those classes.

Fix the course in your mind and your body. Feel the entire course.

THE BOTTOM LINE A big part of riding courses and showing is learning how to sense what the course designer is asking and how he or she is testing the riders.

2010 Hampton Classic

FTI CONSULTING™
Sponsor Since 2005

Class No: 402
$250,000
FTI Grand Prix
1 Jump Off
Sunday,
September 5, 2010

Table: A
Art: 238.2.2
Height: 1.60m

Speed: 375m/min

Length: 515m
T. allowed: 83 sec
T. limit: 166 sec

1st. round: 1 to 13
Efforts: 16

Jump-off:

2-15-7a-7b-9-11-16-13

Length: 335m
T. allowed: 54 sec
T. limit: 108 sec

Reproduced from original
course map designed by
Guilherme Jorge (BRA)

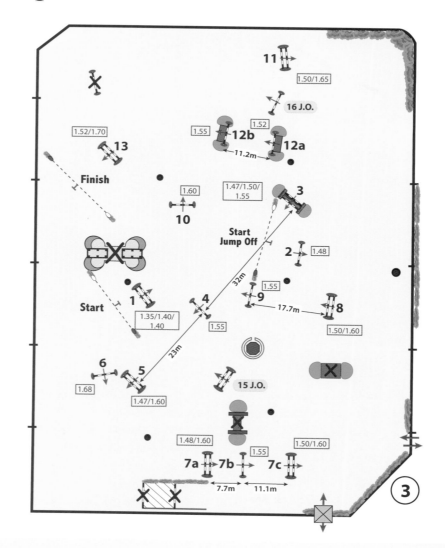

2010 Hampton Classic | Each part of this course distills down to our prime jumping questions and homework. A few examples include a spooky/full jump (#3); a 270-degree rollback on the track from #5 to #6; a short direct line from #8 to #9 and then a long broken line from #9 to #10; and a natural obstacle in the double liverpools (#12a & b). Designed by international course designer Guilherme Jorge, the Hampton Classic Grand Prix is on grass and tests the following:

- Bravery of horse and rider, with the hedge oxer (#3) and the double liverpool (#12a and b)
- Stamina, tested over a long course with many of the most difficult jumping questions asked at the end
- Speed, in that riders had to gallop and make tight turns (a very neat track) to be under the time allowed

1996 Olympic Games
Team Competition

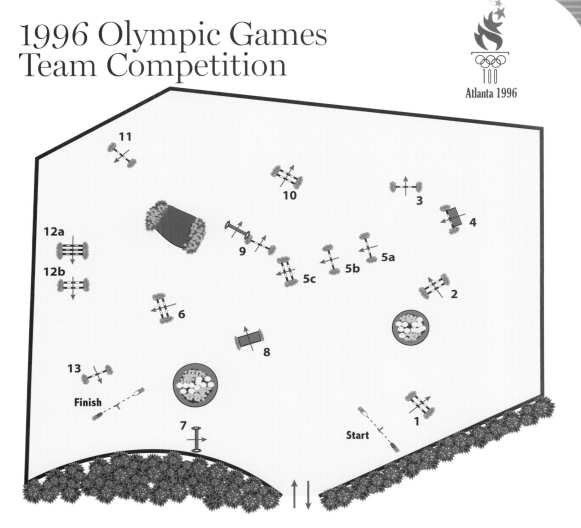

Table: A art.339; Speed: 400m; Time allowed: 93 sec; Distance: 620m; Time Limit: 186 sec

Jump Off; 2, 3, 4, 10, 12ab, 13; Speed: 400m; Time allowed: 53 sec; Distance: 350m; Time Limit: 106 sec

Reproduced from original course map designed by Linda Allen USA "O"

Nations Cup | The moment I saw this diagram, I only saw déjà vu moments as I have trained myself to do all my life. The course started with a staple of my training program – an "S" line over jumps 1, 2, and 3 – then went to a rollback to a gymnastic-like straight line comprising an open-faced liverpool (#4), direct to the Kentucky Barnyard triple combination (#5a, b, c), direct to a large square oxer (#6). Next came a chance to make time to a single jump, the Mt. Rushmore Wall (#7) ; then a left turn away from home to a bending line to a direct line: a wide-open water jump (#8) to a skinny airy gate (#9) to the Taos, New Mexico, wide, square oxer (#10). Another left turn to the last three questions: a bending line from the California Life Guard Beach Tower vertical (#11) to a triple bar/oxer combination (#12a, b) to another soft bending line to the final vertical NASA Space Shuttle (#13). What a great feeling to have déjà vu confidence while taking the test of my life!

You must be able to recognize the overarching question being asked of you and your horse. So watch as many trips in as many classes as you can, across disciplines. Watch how the questions may seem similar but ride differently. Watch how questions that seem very different actually ride similarly. Watch how different solutions suit different kinds of horses and riders. Watch. Watch. Watch. If you can get a person with a seasoned eye to sit, watch, and discuss questions with you, even better.

Hang out on the rail, not just of the show ring, but of the warm-up ring and the back gate. You can learn a lot from watching trainers warm up their riders. Listen to trainers explaining the challenges and questions to their riders and to riders debriefing after their trips.

Here Comes the Déjà Vu

Study. Learn. Do your homework. Deliberately watch the questions that are posed for other riders at the show. By the time your own class comes around, the course and its questions will feel familiar. It will feel like déjà vu.

And for your own course, after you break it down into pieces and have identified the questions, think about how the course will feel as you connect the questions. As you walk the course, try to visualize the feeling of each answer — what balance you need to have, how you'll move your body, and so on. Then, after walking the course, close your eyes and feel how the entire course is going to ride.

try this

Here are some ways to do your homework about courses:

Subscribe to *www.phelpssports.com*, and review the course maps they post for the different horse shows. Look carefully at them, and read the coverage of a range of different classes at different horse shows. You'll start to recognize the names of course designers, and you'll be able to learn from the descriptions of the different courses.

Identify an upcoming class at a well-publicized horse show that will be webcast by a service such as *www.equestrianlife.com*. Watch the class and take notes on what you think the course designer might have been trying to accomplish with the design.

Follow press coverage of the event to read what the course designers and reporters say about the course. Two good sites are *www.chronofhorse.com* and *www.equisearch.com*.

Warm Up and Ace the Test

Even if something doesn't go the way you want, you have to keep going.

WARMING UP IS A CRITICAL part of any horse show. If you watch what happens in the warm-up area, you'll see that everyone takes a different approach. For some, it's about what they as riders want to focus on. For others it's about what helps their horses the most.

Should you or your horse not feel the way you planned on the day of a competition, don't panic. Don't overreact; just simplify your game plan, draw confidence from all the training you did at home, and trust your instincts to ride the horse that is underneath you at the moment.

We tell our riders that warming up is about simplicity. In fact, our mantra is **KISS: Keep It Super Simple**. The following fundamentals are at the core of that approach:

- Don't try anything new or try to learn anything new.

- Have a confident, simple warm-up – keep it plain vanilla.

- Taste a little piece of the key questions.

- Draw on the training you've done at home.

- Focus on your strengths.

We realize that those fundamentals may fall into the "easier said than done" category. But try them. Make them *your* mantras, and you'll be surprised about how much better

KISS: Keep It Super Simple!

THE BOTTOM LINE Knowing how an effective warm-up helps your performance and remembering a few key recommendations for the ring will help you ace the test of any horse show class.

things will go for you in the ring. Remember, the more you worry about doing things right, the worse they may go.

Time to Ace the Test

Acing the test involves patience and focus. You have to focus mentally, emotionally, and physically to give your best show ring performance. The way in which you "get in the zone" is personal. There may be one key ingredient or it may be a medley of things that help you find that zone on demand.

Here are five specific actions that can help you get in your zone and stay there while jumping a course:

- Visualize

- Imitate

- Hear

- Feel

- Identify

Visualize Your Course

Think about what the course is going to look like going through all parts of it. Feel yourself riding the questions; sticking to the track you know is right; committing to the ride that you know will give your horse the opportunity to do his job well. See in your mind what it will

Focus on the Basics

When you're warming up before a class, focus on these basics:

1. Make sure your horse's body is physically loosened and warmed up on the flat. Confirm that he is accepting and listening to your aids.

2. In the first part of your school, concentrate on the simple goals of going straight and forward.

3. At some point, "taste" one or two of the key jumping questions presented in your class.

4. Pause for a moment to review your plan before entering the ring.

And finally, remember to taste the simplicity. Don't overdo it.

look like going around all parts of that course, so that when you're out there, it will feel like déjà vu.

Imitate Someone You Admire

Imagine the rider type and talent that your riding style tends to match, whether it's McLain Ward or Beezie Madden or Scott Stewart or Jessica Springsteen. Imagine how they stretch up, picture how they wait with their bodies, remember their quiet elegance as they accurately gallop around a course. Imitate that when you go out there. Use the image of that top rider to guide your performance on course.

Hear Your Horse's Rhythm

Hear the hoofbeats of your horse's canter and jumping from a natural stride. Hear the blowing of his breath. Think about how what you hear on the way to the first jump is the same as what you heard in the warm-up and what you hear at home. Those sounds confirm that everything is right, that you're okay, and that your ride is going to be good.

Feel Your Horse's Performance

Before you mount up to compete, find a quiet place to close your eyes and feel yourself ride the course, complete with what you're going to see, what you want your horse to feel like underneath you and across the ground, and what you are going to do with your body and weight distribution around the entire course. Feel your horse's energy wanting to head to the next line, to do his job. Feel the track, feel the stride. Feel yourself in balance with your horse, ready to carry out your mission to nail this course. Feel that "just right" ride.

Identify Ace Moments

Whether in hunter, equitation, or jumper classes, you know there are one or two questions in any competition that play to your strength. Perhaps it is a long six on the outside line in the hunter class and you know your horse has a long stride and can walk the line and not lose his form. Maybe you and your equitation horse consistently land on the correct lead and can do the S-line in your class better and smoother than everyone else. It might be that you

and your jumper can turn tighter than your competition and that rollback in the jump-off will give you the chance to win.

try this

- Give yourself some mock competition **experience at home.**

- Set an appropriate course, **one that you haven't practiced.**

- Walk the course, **plan your ride, get in the zone, and deliberately try the steps outlined above.**

- Pick one jump **to warm up on, then leave the ring.**

- Wait at the in gate **as you do a final review in your mind.**

- Enter the ring **as if you were at a show and compete.**

THE CONCEPT IN ACTION: Keeping It Super Simple | Olympic Team Gold and Team Silver medalist **Leslie Howard** is one of the top riders at keeping her show ride simple. By riding straight, forward, left and right, (and fast), Leslie wins again and again. While Leslie does as much homework as the next Olympian, when she goes in the ring she puts the classroom aside and "keeps it super simple" in the ring – she lets her homework carry over into her winning show ring rides. Leslie is a wonderful example of one who rides off instinct – gallop fast first and worry about number of strides later. Horses understand simple, and Leslie understands horses. When you feel like your head is swimming in too much detail remember one of Leslie's secrets: "Keep it simple and just jump the jumps." Here she is pictured riding Jeans Glove Varnel in Wellington, Florida.

Will Simpson on Carlsson vom Doch right after clinching the Team Gold for the United States at the Beijing Olympics 2008

10 | Seeking the Medal

You need to be prepared to compete and win. There is an art to preparing well.

WHAT MAKES SOME PEOPLE win all the time? How do Beezie Madden, McLain Ward, Scott Stewart, Louise Serio, and Jessica Springsteen win consistently and make it look easy?

When something is done at the highest level, it looks easy; it transcends exercise and exertion — it becomes **an art form**. We've talked about riding as an art, and perfecting that art is the way to the top of the field.

But it's not just art. **It's also a lot of very hard work.** A lot of hours of practice and competition. A lot of dedication. That, combined with a special know-how about the nuances that produce the winning ride. Riding and winning at the top is about delivering those nuances when it counts, on the big day. There are many nuances of riding and jumping gained through a lifetime of practice and competition that the average rider isn't aware of. If you watch carefully and really look, you will see and appreciate the little things that make a big difference. We discuss these nuances in more detail in Seeking the Medal 10.3 (see page 188).

The art of
riding is about
the nuances.

In addition to delivering the nuances, top winning riders know how to identify the competitive landscape and plan for maximum success. As you seek to find your "medals," whether that means at an actual competition or in a more metaphorical way, it's important to realize that you have a year-round job. You must target your goals not just for an individual season, but over a multi-year period.

Be proactive about preparing all year-round. Reaching for a specific medal, meaning that you have your eye on a goal that requires entering a series of different competitions, calls for a different mind-set from just sporadically showing in shows as the opportunity arises. (There's nothing wrong at all with taking that path — it's just that competing seriously requires a different mind-set.)

What's your medal?

In this chapter we talk about riding at the top levels with a medal-seeking mind-set. First, you need to be able to answer the question, "What's my medal?" Is it "a capital-M Medal," as in the ASPCA-Maclay Championship or a Marshall & Sterling championship? Is it a championship in your discipline? Or is it a more general "medal" such as "compete in at least three A-level shows this season?"

Medals, Derbies, Classics, and More

Have the top competitions, the highlights, on your radar screen. Set your sights on them and work backward to hit those targets.

CERTAIN TYPES OF CLASSES, divisions, and shows represent the elite athletes of the hunter and equitation divisions. They are called medals, indoors, derbies, and classics and need specific registrations. They also require association membership and impose certain limitations. They are all different, with their own attributes and suitability for specific types of horses and riders. Here's a quick description of each.

The Medals

Medal classes are the pinnacle of equitation for adult and amateur riders. These classes are held at different hunter/jumper shows. You accumulate points throughout the year to qualify for the finals. There are medal classes at the schooling show level as well as at the C, B, and A levels, so even if you're just starting your medal career, you can usually find a series of medals to compete in.

When people say they are "Medal riders" they typically mean that they are junior equitation riders riding in the "Big Eq" divisions — the 3' 6" equitation divisions at the A and AA shows. The three most talked about Medals for America's top junior riders are the ASPCA Maclay, the

---

THE BOTTOM LINE Planning for highlight competitions helps you reach your goal. Identify your target goal and plan backward from there to reach it.

USEF Medal, and the USET Talent Search. Points for these are accumulated over the year by competing in the classes at single shows.

There are also the Washington International Horse Show Equitation Classic and the North American Equitation Championship at Capital Challenge. There are other Big Eq championships for juniors as well — for example, there's a George Morris Excellence in Equitation class at Wellington and the Ronnie Mutch Equitation Championships in Ocala, Florida, and Thermal, California, each year.

The United States Equestrian Federation (USEF) has "tests" that can be used in equitation courses as workoffs between finalists. For example, Test 16 in the 2010 USEF rule book requires riders to change horses. Test 19 is "Demonstration ride of approximately one minute. Rider must advise judge beforehand what ride he plans to demonstrate." Other tests include riding and jumping without stirrups, counter-cantering, and other questions that test rider skill and horse obedience.

While the Big Eq divisions are a wonderful target to aim for, many

Medal, medal — What's the Difference?

There are medals with a *little m*, and then there are the Medals with a *big M*. Most medal classes have a sponsor name attached to them — it can be either a for-profit organization or a nonprofit organization. For example, the Maclay medal class is actually the ASPCA-Maclay Medal.

On the West Coast there is the Onadarka Medal for children ages 12 and under. Each Medal class has its own rules, course requirements, and criteria for entering, so it's important to know which medal you're riding in.

people are better off at the 2' 9" or 3' 0" medals. There are quite a number of opportunities out there to ride in medal classes at this level, for both children and adults. Both Ariat and Marshall & Sterling sponsor a number of medals for these groups, so check show prize lists or the company websites to find out where a show near you may be holding these medals.

Check the rulebooks. Know the rules and tests for every class.

The Indoors

"The Indoors" refers to the regional and national Medal finals and championship shows that occur in the fall each year. Examples are the Pessoa/ USEF Medal Finals in Harrisburg, Pennsylvania, the Washington International Horse Show (WIHS) Medal in Washington, D.C., and the Ariat National Adult Medal Finals, which takes place at the Capital Challenge horse show in Maryland.

The Derbies

Derbies are special competitions with long courses that include natural obstacles. There are hunter derbies and jumper derbies; the idea behind these classes is that the obstacles and questions posed mimic those found riding through the countryside. They may take place on grass fields or in an arena and often involve more fences than a simple hunter or jumper course does. It takes a special horse to compete in Derbies, one with an appetite for big jumps, natural obstacles, and long courses.

The Classics

Classics are the highlight competition at a show for hunters, equitation riders, and jumpers. A classic is the most coveted class at each level and is usually the hardest. The competition is held over two rounds, both of which count. The scoring is usually numeric and the combined total score from both rounds determines the winner.

Typically, the entry fee is higher for classics, and money is paid back to the winners — sometimes very large amounts. Hunter classic riders often wear shadbelly coats — hunt coats that are longer in the back and cut away at the stomach.

A classic that is held for the most advanced jumpers and is open to professionals is call a Grand Prix. Usually the purse size and jump heights determines if the jumper classic is called a Grand Prix.

try this

Visit *www.medalmaclay.com* and look at the equitation courses.
See if you can identify all the elements we talked about in chapters 8 and 9. Consider what the course designer and judges are looking for. Then find a medal class at a horse show nearby, and watch the class carefully — see if you can pick the top four!

Test Your Eye

Make the first round of an equitation course by numbering jumps on the opposite page from 1 to 10. Then create a second-round test of about six obstacles, again by numbering the jumps. As you design your first-round course, include the six prime jumping questions asked below and when designing the second round include the five "test" questions.

Note the following: Each jump can be jumped only once and all obstacles can be jumped in either direction in both the first round and the test. For the test, assume that any jump can be lowered to the correct height for the trot jump.

FIRST ROUND JUMPING QUESTIONS
- Direct line
- Spooky jump
- Roll back
- Inside turn*
- Combination
- S line

*This means to ride a shorter track by turning in front of an obstacle rather than going around it to approach the next jump in the course.

SECOND ROUND TEST QUESTIONS
- Trot a jump
- Halt
- Counter canter a jump
- Gallop a jump
- Execute a flying change

Peter's answer to the Test Your Eye challenge is shown in appendix 1 on pages 192–193.

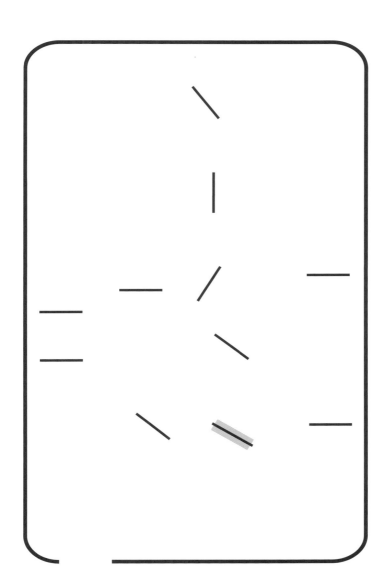

Planning Your Show Year

Showing competitively is really about managing two careers — yours as a rider and your horse's as a show horse.

AS WITH ANY GOAL, achieving your "medal" involves careful planning. It requires that you have a different perspective of time — you need to **think in terms of years**. As part of your plan, ask yourself the following questions:

1. What are my goals for my riding? For my horse?

2. Where do I need to be with my riding to achieve those goals?

3. How far away is that from where I am currently?

4. Where does my horse need to be to achieve those goals?

5. How far away is his training now from those goals?

6. What are the steps to get to my goals?

7. What does that mean for this year?

Let's pause for a minute and look at Lisa, who has been taking lessons for several years with her 12-year-old Thoroughbred gelding. For the past two years, she has competed in three or four shows a year, mostly in equitation. She placed in a couple of classes but usually doesn't finish in the ribbons. With a full-time job and a limited budget, she needs to plan carefully. Here are her answers to the above questions.

THE BOTTOM LINE Plan your horse show season carefully to increase your odds of success but more importantly, to keep your horse sound.

1. I want to win a Championship Medal in Adult Equitation. My goal for my horse is the same.

2. I need to be more consistent in my approach to the fences and stay focused on the track I've chosen.

3. I'm not too far from my goal, as I jump well at home but get nervous and lose my focus after about six jumps in the show ring.

4. My horse is capable of going well if I ride him well. He needs to build trust in my ability to guide him around the course.

5. If I can keep my focus and be consistent, he will do what I ask.

6. I need to feel more comfortable at shows. To reach my goal I need to accumulate enough points to qualify for a championship class.

7. For this year I should look for one-day shows where I can enter several classes and get the most practice possible at each one.

Once these kinds of questions are answered, the next thing is to actually do the planning. Lisa decides to focus on shows where (a) her trainer can ride her horse in a warm-up class to give him a solid, consistent ride; (b) there is another class that Lisa could do for schooling and practice; and (c) she can enter the medal class in the afternoon.

She combs show prize lists in November to begin planning her season. She carefully identifies the shows that meet her criteria, then fills her calendar with the shows she'll do to maximize her chances at accumulating enough points to qualify for the adult-class medal she's after.

The Nuances of a Winning Ride

Learn from the masters of our sport.
Learn the nuances of the art of riding.

THE NUANCES THAT winning riders know and use in their riding are so subtle that they're difficult to see at first glance. In general winning riders have the ability to do a number of complicated things all at the same time:

- Stay focused and composed

- Deliver the ride with confidence

- Be both a horseman and a competitor

- Deal with the unexpected and the imperfect

Stay Focused and Composed

Focus. The ability to focus is one of the most critical differentiators between those who win and those who don't.

Focusing is the ability to block out any distractions as you prepare to and then enter the ring. It enables you to consider only your horse and the task at hand and nothing else, and it requires a tremendous amount of discipline. Top riders focus on their rides and let nothing come between their concentration and execution.

Composure. Although clearly related to focusing, the ability to maintain composure is about mental and physical poise. It means an ability to remain calm no matter what comes your way and to carry on despite unexpected events. A composed rider has a unique grace about her and a high degree of self-control and presence. You won't see riders with this ability ever taking their anger out

THE BOTTOM LINE Understand the subtle nuances that underlie winning rides so you can incorporate them as appropriate for you and your horse.

on their horses or acting distraught in the ring. Top riders always, always, always remain composed.

Deliver the Ride with Confidence

Confidence. Top riders believe in themselves, their horses, and their rides, and it shows in the ring. Their confidence comes from the knowledge they've gained over a tremendous number of hours of preparation and training. It also comes from their sense of self and their identity as top athletes. Top riders harness that confidence and convey it to their horses. Never doubting themselves or their mounts results in clear and purposeful efforts in the ring and significantly helps their ability to focus and win.

Recognize and strategize. Riding at the top levels involves superior skills in thinking strategically. It requires that riders recognize the initial questions of the course and understand how the competition changes as the class progresses. Top riders have a repertoire of strategies to respond to the dynamic nature of the challenge at hand. Knowing the best answer for the situation they're facing with their particular horse sets these riders apart.

Know your strengths. Top riders know their own strengths. They select their mounts and their competitions to set the stage for success based on their strengths. Operating in this manner takes careful and honest reflection plus confirmation from your immediate support team.

Deliver the ride. All the competition experience and skills in the world don't equal a champion rider until you add the most important attribute — the learned or innate ability to win when it matters most, whether that means a critical clear round, putting in the highest score in a hunter classic, or nailing the test in the Maclay Finals.

Always keep your cool in the ring — ride with confidence!

Be a Horseman *and* a Competitor

Know your horse's strengths. As an overall horse person, a top rider knows her horse's strengths and how to play to those strengths. She strategizes to make sure each ride highlights her horse's best abilities. She creates her plans and selects the shows she'll attend accordingly, always seeking to build on her horse's strong points.

Bring out the best in your horse. Every top ride has a sixth sense developed from years of experience that allows her to know always right where her horse is, both mentally and physically. This insight allows her to bring out the best in her horse and to guide him to a peak performance. This sense is a clear reflection of the special bonds that form between horse and rider at this level, allowing the rider to operate almost as an extension of her mount. Top riders anticipate how their horses will react to a given competition question.

Manage your horse physically and emotionally. As a complete, all-

A winning performance is the result of the relationship between horse and rider that develops from their years of experience together.

around horse person, a winning rider knows how to manage all aspects of her horse's physical and emotional health. Her expert eye for subtle changes in her horse's moods and well-being allows her to note if plans for conditioning are on or off track. Careful planning allows her to train and condition a horse purposefully so he'll peak just in time for the big competitions.

The ability to accomplish this is the result of years and years of education, openness to learning, and experience. Because these top riders are so good at reading their horses, they often modify their competition day warm-up or show ring plan to adapt to the ever-changing temperament or health of the horse and the conditions of that day.

Balance freshness with preparation.
Knowing her horse well allows a top rider to balance the freshness needed for a big competition with the daily preparation necessary to hone her skills. These riders understand that there is such a thing as being over-prepared, and they use their vast experience to keep their horses just right for competition — fresh enough to go into the ring with bright eyes and a careful jump but not so fresh they don't pay attention to their riders. The ability to take your horse in to the ring with this correct balance is *huge*! It can mean the difference between success and failure.

Deal with the Unexpected and the Imperfect

Because of their ability to maintain focus and composure, top riders are masterful at taking an imperfect moment or unexpected situation and making it work out. They are unfazed by an umbrella blowing across the field or a dog running through the ring. A less-than-perfect situation such as an inordinately deep distance is ridden as though it's a perfect spot, with the body invisibly adding leg to support and help the horse exit the situation gracefully.

Top riders downplay the drama and highlight the strong points. And they make quick but well-grounded decisions to make weaker moments work. Nobody rides perfectly every competition. Every rider sometimes goes a bit too deep or a bit too long. The top riders find a way to get it done and go clear! We hope this book helps you to "go clear" as well — to meet your goals and achieve your dreams!

You'll be a better competitor by being a horseman first and striving to bring out the best in your horse.

Test Your Eye

Peter's answer to the Test Your Eye challenge on pages 184–185 is shown on the opposite page. He identified the six prime jumping questions as follows:

- Direct line   #2 to #3
- Spooky jump   #9
- Rollback   From #6 to #7
- Inside turn   From #1 to #2
- Combination   #8a and 8b
- S line   #4 to #5 to #6

THE TEST THAT PETER DEVISED IS THIS:

- Canter   #1, #2, and #10
- Halt
- Counter canter   #5R (take jump 5 in reverse direction)
- Trot   #4R (trot jump 4 in reverse direction)
- Gallop   #6
- Demonstrate a flying lead change going toward the out gate

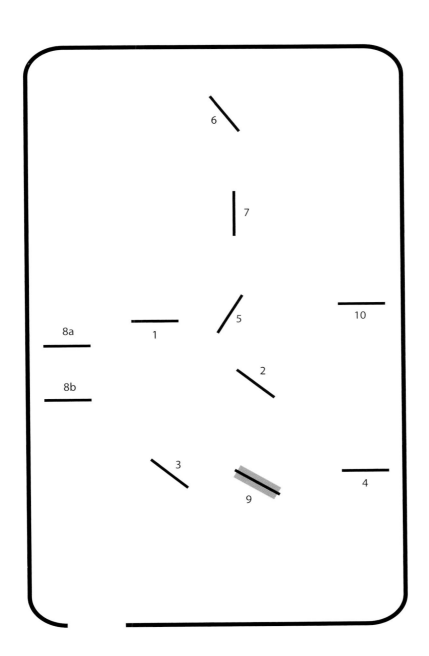

Olympic Medals in Show Jumping
Team Competition

	GOLD	SILVER	BRONZE
1912 STOCKHOLM	Sweden	France	Germany
1920 ANTWERP	Sweden	Belgium	Italy
1924 PARIS	Sweden	Switzerland	Portugal
1928 AMSTERDAM	Spain	Poland	Sweden
1932 LOS ANGELES	No nation completed the course with three riders.		
1936 BERLIN	Germany	Netherlands	Portugal
1948 LONDON	Mexico	Spain	Great Britain
1952 HELSINKI	Great Britain	Chile	**United States** William Steinkraus and Hollandia Arthur McCashin and Miss Budweiser John William Russell and Democrat
1956 STOCKHOLM	Germany	Italy	Great Britain
1960 ROME	Germany	**United States** Frank Chapot and Trail Guide William Steinkraus and Ksar d'Esprit George H. Morris and Sinjon	Italy
1964 TOKYO	Germany	France	Italy
1968 MEXICO CITY	Canada	France	West Germany
1972 MUNICH	West Germany	**United States** William Steinkraus and Main Spring Neal Shapiro and Sloopy Kathryn Kusner and Fleet Apple Frank Chapot and White Lightning	Italy
1976 MONTREAL	France	West Germany	Belgium
1980 MOSCOW	Soviet Union	Poland	Mexico
1980 ALTERNATE GAMES, ROTTERDAM	Canada	Great Britain	Austria

	GOLD	SILVER	BRONZE
1984 LOS ANGELES	**United States** Joseph Fargis and Touch of Class Conrad Homfeld and Abdullah Leslie Howard and Albany Melanie Smith and Calypso	Great Britain	West Germany
1988 SEOUL	West Germany	**United States** Greg Best and Gem Twist Lisa Ann Jacquin and For the Moment Anne Kursinski and Starman Joseph Fargis and Mill Pearl	France
1992 BARCELONA	Netherlands	Austria	France
1996 ATLANTA	Germany	**United States** Peter Leone and Legato Leslie Burr-Howard and Extreme Anne Kursinski and Eros Michael R. Matz and Rhum	Brazil
2000 SYDNEY	Germany	Switzerland	Brazil
2004 ATHENS	**United States** Peter Wylde and Fein Cera McLain Ward and Sapphire Beezie Madden and Authentic Chris Kappler and Royal Kaliber	Sweden	Germany
2008 BEIJING	**United States** McLain Ward on Sapphire Laura Kraut on Cedric Will Simpson on Carlsson vom Dach Beezie Madden on Authentic	Canada	Switzerland

Individual Competition *(U.S. competitors only)*

1932 LOS ANGELES	Silver	Harry Chamberlin on Show Girl
1968 MEXICO CITY	Gold	William Steinkraus on Snowbound
1972 MUNICH	Bronze	Neal Shapiro and Sloopy
1980 ALTERNATE **GAMES, ROTTERDAM**	Bronze	Melanie Smith on Calypso
1984 LOS ANGELES	Gold	Joseph Fargis on Touch of Class
	Silver	Conrad Homfeld on Abdullah
1988 SEOUL	Silver	Greg Best on Gem Twist
1992 BARCELONA	Bronze	Norman Dello Joio on Irish
2004 ATHENS	Silver	Chris Kappler on Royal Kaliber
2008 BEIJING	Bronze	Beezie Madden on Authentic

Show Jumping World Championships

The Show Jumping World Championships are now held every four years as part of the World Equestrian Games. Individual competition started in 1953, with team competition being added in 1978.

TEAM COMPETITION

1978 AACHEN: Great Britain

1982 DUBLIN: France

1986 AACHEN: United States of America
    Michael Matz and Chef
    Conrad Homfeld and Abdullah
    Katie Monahan and Amadia
    Katharine Burdsall and The Natural

1990 STOCKHOLM: France

1994 DEN HAAG: Germany

1998 ROME: Germany

2002 JEREZ DE LA FRONTERA: France

2006 AACHEN: Netherlands

2010 LEXINGTON: Germany

INDIVIDUAL COMPETITION (GOLD, SILVER, BRONZE)

1953 PARIS — Spain, West Germany, France

1954 MADRID — West Germany, France, Spain

1955 AACHEN — West Germany, Italy, United Kingdom

1956 AACHEN — Italy, Spain, West Germany

1960 VENEZIA — Italy, Argentina, United Kingdom

1966 BUENOS AIRES — France, Spain, Italy

1970 LA BAULE — United Kingdom, Italy, United Kingdom

1974 HICKSTEAD — West Germany, Ireland, Austria

1978 AACHEN — West Germany, Ireland, **United States** (Michael Matz on Jet Run)

1982 DUBLIN — West Germany, United Kingdom, France

1986 AACHEN — Canada, **United States** (Conrad Homfeld on Abdullah), United Kingdom

1990 STOCKHOLM — France, United Kingdom, France

1994 THE HAGUE — West Germany, France, Germany

1998 ROME — Brazil, France, Germany

2002 JEREZ DE LA FRONTERA — Ireland, France, **United States** (Peter Wylde on Fein Cera)

2006 AACHEN — Belgium, **United States** (Beezie Madden on Authentic), Germany

2010 LEXINGTON — Germany, Saudi Arabia, Canada

National Horse Show ASPCA Maclay Championship Finals

This competition for junior riders is held annually at the National Horse Show at the end of the indoor season.

1933	Audrey Hasler	**1961**	Bernie Traurig	**1991**	Peter Lutz
1934	Elizabeth Hyland Molony	**1962**	Carol Altman	**1992**	Nicole Shahinian
1935	Lillian M. Chambers Lindemann	**1963**	Wendy Mairs	**1993**	Kelley Farmer
		1964	Lane Schultz	**1994**	Leslie Fishback
1936	Ellie Wood P.K. Baxter	**1965**	Chrystine Jones	**1995**	Megan Johnstone
1937	Walton Perry Davis, Jr.	**1966**	Debbie Wilson Jenkins	**1996**	Lauren Bass
1938	Archie Dean, Jr.	**1967**	Conrad Homefeld	**1997**	Keri Kampsen
1939	Hugh Dean	**1968**	Brooke Hodgson	**1998**	Erynn Ballard
1940	James Thomas, Jr.	**1970**	Fred Bauer	**1999**	Emily Williams
1941	William C. Steinkraus	**1971**	Anna Jane White	**2000**	Avery Dimmig
1942	William P. Dunn, III	**1972**	Leslie Burr	**2001**	Brian Walker
1943	Anne Morningstar	**1973**	Michael Patrick	**2002**	Erin Stewart
1944	Alice Babcock	**1974**	Alex Dunaif	**2003**	Mathew Sereni
1945	Nancy Dean	**1975**	Katharine Burdsall	**2004**	Megan Young
1946	Elaine Moore	**1976**	Collette Lozins	**2005**	Brianne Goutal
1947	Frank Chapot	**1977**	Francie Steinwedell	**2006**	Maggie McAlary
1948	Charlotte Hanlon	**1978**	Michael Sasso	**2007**	Kimberly McCormack
1949	Myrna Jackson Felvy	**1979**	Gary Young	**2008**	Jessica Springsteen
1950	Mary Gay Huffard	**1980**	Laura Tidball	**2009**	Zazou Hoffman
1951	G. Baker Schroeder, Jr.	**1981**	Lisa Castellucci	**2010**	Hayley Barnhill
1952	George Morris	**1982**	Peter Wylde	**2011**	Sarah Milliren
1953	Glena Lee Maduro	**1983**	Linda Kossick		
1954	Ronnie Martini	**1984**	Francesca Mazella		
1955	Wilson Dennehy	**1985**	Steve Heinicke		
1956	Barbara Friedemann	**1986**	Scott Hofstetter		
1957	J. Michael Plumb	**1987**	Stacia Klein		
1958	Wendy Hanson	**1988**	Christy Conrad		
1959	Hank Minchin	**1989**	Raymond Texel		
1960	Mary Mairs	**1990**	Lauren Kay		

Road to the Olympics

ADAPTED FROM

Unbridled Passion
by Jeffery Powpas
Acanthus Publishing 2011
(used with permission)

AN EXTRAORDINARY partnership exists between an Olympic horse and rider. A special union is forged during the months and years that bring them along the sometimes bumpy road to the Grand Prix arena in an Olympic stadium. The rider must be physically fit, extremely dedicated, very talented, and totally trusting of the horse. The horse must be up to the sport physically and mentally, and must have that magical ability to perform flawlessly time and time again. A horse like that is called a "Sunday horse" — one that is prepared to compete internationally in the biggest 1.60 m classes.

No one understands or appreciates this more than Peter Leone. A true gentleman and an athlete, he is both gracious and passionate when discussing his partnership with Legato and the road that led to their selection for the 1996 Olympic Games.

Peter's trip to the 1996 Games began in the early '90s, when his hopes and dreams were suddenly centered on the four-year-old gelding he found in Belgium. Because it was raining, Peter had to ride Legato for the first time in a tiny indoor ring, but he knew after just one fence that the horse was all talent. For a large horse, Legato came off the ground like a bird and he knew exactly where his legs were. Peter could feel Legato's confidence and intelligence; he had the look of a winner.

Getting Acclimated

Peter brought Legato home to his family's Ri-Arm Farm in New Jersey. "I didn't jump him for four months after I got him home," Peter says. "Now with most people, that's the first thing they do. I saw no point in jumping him as that was the easy part for Legato. I brought him along slowly and put all the pieces in place on the flat and then spent a lot of time introducing him to gymnastics."

Peter, who is known for his patience and kindness as a trainer, let Legato tell him when he was ready. By the time the horse was six, he was Peter's number two horse on the U.S. team in Italy, earning ribbons in every class they entered. He was turning out to be everything Peter had hoped for.

A Bump in the Road

One Monday morning, while at his then job as national sales director of Liberty Travel, Peter got an emergency call. Legato had been seriously injured during the night, when he became cast in his stall and a splinter of wood lodged in his stifle joint. After surgery, the young horse was stuck in his stall for 90 days playing with a rubber ball. Once Legato had healed enough to start working lightly under saddle, Peter put him on a carefully regimented schedule, beginning with 60 days of riding at the walk.

By the time the Winter Equestrian Festival began in Wellington, Florida, Legato was eight and not yet in his prime. As Peter recalls, "I went in my first Grand Prix, which is a World Cup down there, and he jumped it freakishly well. He was double clear! Bringing him back from a career-ending injury was a real journey."

Later that year, Peter began to realize that he and Legato had a shot at the 1996 Olympics. He carefully planned his competition schedule so that the horse had a taste of competing in Europe, riding him at the Dublin Horse Show and the Nations Cup in Aachen, and winning both the World Cup Grand Prix at South Hampton and the World Cup Grand Prix in the famed Devon Oval.

Setbacks — Minor and Major

As is often the case in show jumping, it was Peter's turn to sustain an injury, breaking the fifth metacarpal in his hand, which was enough to interfere with riding. Joe Fargis, a fellow rider and 1984 Olympic gold medalist, introduced Peter to his surgeon, Dr. Charles Virgin, who told Peter he would get him back in the saddle so that he would not even be thinking about his injured hand. Peter and Legato completed the first two trials successfully and were in third place at the end.

In addition to riding Legato, Peter was bringing along several green horses. In a jump-off at the Garden State Horse Show, his young mount flipped over a vertical, driving Peter into the ground and shattering his collarbone 48 hours before the third Olympic trial. In the ambulance, Peter told his wife, Marcella, "Get me to Dr. Virgin!" He missed the third trial but, with five screws in place, prepared to compete in the remaining ones, just two weeks away at the Old Salem Horse Show.

To help make the Olympic dream come true, Team Leone sprang into action. Brother Armand, a doctor and a lawyer, managed a myriad of details. Brother Mark, also an international Grand Prix rider, kept Legato fit and ready to compete. Peter knew that even with hard work, he would just barely be able

to make it to the trials and he would still be in a great deal of pain. Under FEI rules, competitors could not take any painkillers.

Playing by the Rules

What was permissible was to locally infiltrate the fracture site, meaning Peter could recive injections of numbing agents directly into his collarbone. Permission was granted for Peter to ride without a jacket because it was so painful to pull it over his shoulder. After Peter and his brothers walked the course, Armand drove Peter to a nearby hospital for the approved injections. Mark warmed up Legato, and Peter put in a four-fault round. Two hours later, the injection had worn off and the pain interfered with Peter's ride, resulting in an unusual 12-fault score. This was his second discard; he had no more room for error.

Peter rode the next four trials with an anesthesiologist on the grounds to numb his injury right before his ride; he wound up one clear round away from making the Olympic team. At the last trial, held three weeks later at the historic USET headquarters in Gladstone, New Jersey, Peter was able to warm up his own horse, though he still rode with a numbed shoulder. The dynamic pair had a magnificent clear round and won the final trial, earning themselves a berth on the Olympic team.

Team USA

At the Olympics just six weeks later, Peter rode without any medical help. Legato was with him the whole time, boosting his confidence and helping him move past the pain every step of the way. "I took care of Legato when he was badly hurt and he did the same for me when I was in need," he says. It was magical how Legato sensed Peter's compromised condition and made up for his weakened state, carrying him to clear rounds and an Olympic dream.

The Germans took the gold in those Games and United States won the silver medal in the team competition, with Peter putting in one four-fault round and one clear round. Michael Matz had four faults in both rounds, Anne Kursinski went clear and eight, and Leslie Howard went 14 and clear, leaving Peter's record the best of the U.S. team.

A Second Sunday Horse

Legato was a special, wonderful, perhaps once-in-a-lifetime horse, and he lived the rest of his life in Peter's care. Peter went almost ten years without an extraordinary partner for the biggest rings and venues. But recently he has been blessed again with a real Sunday horse, Select. He started riding the handsome chestnut in 2010, and they went all the way to the Pfizer $1 Million Grand Prix in 2010 and a clear round in the $500,000 Winter Equestrian Festival final class in 2011. Who knows what they'll achieve next?

Team Leone

AS THE STORY of Peter's path to the Olympics makes clear, his journey was a family affair. He was fortunate to have brothers who not only supported him, but knew exactly what he was going through and what he needed to make it work. In fact, younger brother Mark had only just given up his own hopes for a berth on the 1996 team after losing one horse to injury and ending up out of the running with his second horse. He put aside his own disappointment to do what was needed. Armand, the oldest of the three, not only had both legal and medical expertise to offer, he is also an excellent horseman and experienced competitor.

The three boys grew up in Franklin Lakes, New Jersey, taking riding lessons together because their mother, Rita, wanted them to partake in the same activity. The brothers started riding at a nearby barn and then cared for their own horses at their family barn in Oakland. As teenagers they were able to train with George Morris and spent summers going to shows and competing at the highest levels. Armand was the Leading National Rider at Madison Square Garden in 1977, after which he represented the U.S. team for more than a decade. He qualified for the 1980 Olympics and participated in the Alternate Games in Rotterdam that year. Mark won the AHSA Medal finals in 1979 and continued his winning ways by claiming victory in over 25 Grands Prix and riding for the U.S. team for more than 20 years. In 1982, Team Leone, as they had come to be called, qualified for the World Cup finals in Goteburg, Sweden, and a few months later made show-jumping history by being the first all-family Nations Cup team at the CSIO in Lucerne, Switzerland.

Always close, in spite of the normal competitiveness between siblings, when the brothers faced the ultimate test, they called upon their collective and individual strengths, experience, and knowledge of each other to help Peter make the team and medal at the 1996 Olympic Games. Team Leone represented the United States for 30 years, participating in

10 World Cup finals, a World Championships, and an Olympic Games, and scoring victories at every major competition in the United States and most international shows.

All three brothers remain active in show jumping and equestrian sports. Peter and Mark ride and coach professionally, Peter out of Lionshare Farm in Greenwich, Connecticut, and Mark out of the family's original Ri-Arm Farm in Oakland (named for Rita and Armand, Sr.). Armand practices law not far from Ri-Arm farm and is vice president and chairman of the high performance working group for the USEF.

Armand, Peter, and Mark Leone in Quebec City, 1981

Acknowledgments

WE'D LIKE TO DO OUR BEST TO THANK the many people without whose help this book would have never been possible. First and foremost, Deborah Burns, our acquiring editor at Storey. We "dated" Deb and Storey for two full years before we signed our contract, and without her foresight and faith in our goals, it would have never come to fruition. Similarly, without the unwavering help and expertise of our project editor, Lisa Hiley, this book would never have been completed, and certainly wouldn't have turned out as well as it did. Her patience and willingness to work with us and our crazy horse show schedules made a world of difference.

Kenneth Kraus was an absolute godsend in terms of his wonderful, high-quality photos of the top riders throughout the book — it was a treat to work with him on this project. Thanks also go to Nick Granat for his help in providing course maps and photos.

A number of people supported us throughout this journey: The staff and riders at Lionshare Farm deserve a hearty thank you for their extra efforts in covering the business while we were holed up working on the manuscript. Our incredibly supportive spouses and children endured countless hours of our absence and distraction and we offer a whole host of heartfelt thanks for your warmth and love.

Peter would like to thank the other two legs of Team Leone, his brothers Armand and Mark, who serve as sounding boards and invaluable resources in both his professional and personal life.

The students and faculty at the Center for Leadership Studies and the School of Management at Binghamton University, where Kim is a tenured professor of Leadership, offered wonderful support and energy throughout this project.

And finally, we'd like to thank the incredible horsemen and women who have come before us, many of whom we've been lucky enough to learn from and experience their magic firsthand. Kim's foundation as a rider and coach was shaped by Steve Milne and Sue Payne, coach of the Smith College IHSA riding team. Sullivan Davis, George Morris, Frank Chapot, Bert DeNemethy, and Michael Matz all actively influenced Peter's riding, principles, discipline, and understanding of horses and horsemanship.

Index

Page numbers in *italics* indicate illustrations or photographs; those in **bold** indicate tables.

Other Storey Titles You Will Enjoy

These and other books from Storey Publishing are available wherever quality books are sold or by calling 1-800-441-5700.

Visit us at www.storey.com.

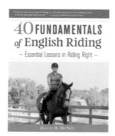

40 Fundamentals of English Riding

HOLLIE H. MCNEIL
In-depth instruction on 40 basic elements essential to all riders interested in the classic riding disciplines of dressage, jumping, and eventing – includes a DVD. 192 pages. Hardcover with jacket. ISBN 978-1-60342-789-0.

101 Jumping Exercises for Horse & Rider

LINDA L. ALLEN WITH DIANNA R. DENNIS
A must-have workbook that provides a logical and consistent series of exercises with easy-to-follow diagrams and instructions for all riding abilities.
240 pages. Paper with comb binding. ISBN 978-1-58017-465-7.

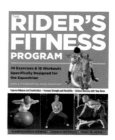

The Rider's Fitness Program

DIANNA R. DENNIS, JOHN J. MCCULLY, AND PAUL M. JURIS
A unique, six-week workout routine to help build the strength, endurance, and skills that will enhance the riding experience.
224 pages. Paper. ISBN 978-1-58017-542-5.

The Rider's Problem Solver

JESSICA JAHIEL
Answers to problems familiar to riders of all levels and styles, from a clinician and equine behavior expert.
384 pages. Paper.
ISBN 978-1-58017-838-9.

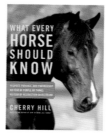

What Every Horse Should Know

CHERRY HILL
A guide to teaching the skills every horse needs to learn to bring out the full potential of the horse-human partnership.
192 pages. Paper.
ISBN 978-1-60342-713-5. Hardcover.
ISBN 978-1-60342-716-6.

Zen Mind, Zen Horse

ALLEN J. HAMILTON, MD
Spiritual principles and practical applications of a chi-based approach to horse-human communication.
320 pages. Paper. ISBN 978-1-60342-565-0.